59 KAGAN STRUCTURES

Proven Engagement Strategies

Dr. Spencer Kagan
Miguel Kagan
Laurie Kagan

Kagan

Kagan

© 2016 by *Kagan Publishing*

Kagan Publishing
981 Calle Amanecer
San Clemente, CA 92673
1 (800) 933-2667
www.KaganOnline.com

ISBN: 978-1-933445-33-5

Kagan Structures
QUICK LOOK

1. AllRecord RoundRobin
2. AllRecord Consensus
3. Centerpiece
4. Fan-N-Pick
5. Dip-A-Strip
6. Fan-N-Pick Partners
7. Flashcard Star
8. Idea RoundUp!
9. Inside-Outside Circle
10. Rotating Lines
11. Instant Star
12. Jot Thoughts
13. Kinesthetic Symbols
14. Listen Right
15. Numbered Heads Together
16. Paired Heads Together
17. Traveling Heads Together
18. Pair Share
19. Paraphrase Passport
20. Quiz-Quiz-Trade
21. Quiz-N-Compare
22. Snowball
23. RallyCoach
24. Mix-Pair-RallyCoach
25. RallyQuiz
26. Traveling RallyQuiz

27. RallyRobin
28. Both Record RallyRobin
29. RallyInterview
30. RallyRead
31. RallyRecall
32. RallyTable
33. RallyTable Consensus
34. Simultaneous RallyTable
35. Read-N-Review
36. RoundRobin
37. Continuous RoundRobin
38. Rotating Role RoundRobin
39. Single RoundRobin
40. Think-Write-RoundRobin
41. Timed RoundRobin
42. RoundTable
43. Continuous RoundTable
44. Pass-N-Praise

45. Rotating Role RoundTable
46. RoundTable Consensus
47. Simultaneous RoundTable
48. Single RoundTable
49. Timed RoundTable
50. Sage-N-Scribe
51. Showdown
52. Similarity Groups
53. Talking Chips
54. Team Interview
55. Timed Pair Share
56. Gossip Gossip
57. Timed Pair Interview
58. Traveling Pair Share
59. Invisible Pal

59 KAGAN STRUCTURES

TABLE OF CONTENTS

TABLE OF CONTENTS continued

Table of Contents

TABLE OF CONTENTS continued

STRUCTURE FUNCTIONS

This dot chart illustrates recommended uses for the structures featured in this book. The structures here represent a subset of the over 200 Kagan Structures.

KEY ★ HIGHLY RECOMMENDED • RECOMMENDED

STRUCTURES	Page	Classbuilding	Teambuilding	Social Skills	Communication Skills	Decision-Making	Knowledgebuilding	Procedure Learning	Processing Info	Thinking Skills	Presentations
			Interpersonal				Academic				
ALLRECORD CONSENSUS	3		★	★	★	★	★	•	•	★	
ALLRECORD ROUNDROBIN	1		★	★	★		★	•	•	★	
BOTH RECORD RALLYROBIN	139			★	★		★	•	★	★	
CENTERPIECE	5		★	★	★		★		★	★	
CONTINUOUS ROUNDROBIN	158		★	★	★		★	•	★	★	
CONTINUOUS ROUNDTABLE	166		★	★	★		★	•	★	★	
DIP-A-STRIP	16		★	★	★		★	★	•	•	
FAN-N-PICK	11		★	★	★		★	★	★	★	
FAN-N-PICK PARTNERS	17			★	★		★	★	★	★	
FLASHCARD STAR	31	★		★	★		★	•			
GOSSIP, GOSSIP	222			★	★				★	★	
IDEA ROUNDUP!	35	★		★	★		★		★	★	
INSIDE-OUTSIDE CIRCLE	39	★		★	★		★	•	★	★	★
INSTANT STAR	61			★	★		•	•	★	★	
INVISIBLE PAL	230	★		★	★		★				★
JOT THOUGHTS	65		★	★	★		•		•	★	
KINESTHETIC SYMBOLS	75						★				
LISTEN RIGHT!	79			★	★		★		•		
MIX-PAIR-RALLYCOACH	129	★		★	★		★	★			
NUMBERED HEADS TOGETHER	87		•	★	★	•	★	★	★	★	
PAIR SHARE	99			★	★				★	★	
PAIRED HEADS TOGETHER	95			★	★	•	★	★	★	★	
PARAPHRASE PASSPORT	103			★	★				★		
PASS-N-PRAISE	166		•	★	★				•	•	
QUIZ-N-COMPARE	116						★	•	•		
QUIZ-QUIZ-TRADE	109	★		★	★		★	•			
RALLYCOACH	123			★	★		•	★			
RALLYINTERVIEW	139			★	★				★	★	★
RALLYQUIZ	133			★	★		★				
RALLYREAD	140			★	★		★				

59 Kagan Structures
Kagan Publishing • 1 (800) 933-2667 • KaganOnline.com

KEY ★ HIGHLY RECOMMENDED • RECOMMENDED

STRUCTURES	Page	Classbuilding	Teambuilding	Social Skills	Communication Skills	Decision-Making	Knowledgebuilding	Procedure Learning	Processing Info	Thinking Skills	Presentations
		Interpersonal					Academic				
RALLYRECALL	140			★	★		★		★		
RALLYROBIN	137			★	★		★	•	★	★	
RALLYTABLE	143			★	★		★	★	★		
RALLYTABLE CONSENSUS	146			★	★		★	★	★		
READ-N-REVIEW	149			★	★		★				
ROTATING LINES	46			★	★		★	•	★	★	★
ROTATING ROLE ROUNDROBIN	159			★	★		★	★	★	★	
ROTATING ROLE ROUNDTABLE	167			★	★		★	★	★	★	
ROUNDROBIN	153		★	★	★		★	•	★	★	★
ROUNDTABLE	162		★	★	•		★	•	•	★	
ROUNDTABLE CONSENSUS	168		★	★	★	★	★	•	★	★	
SAGE-N-SCRIBE	171			★	★		★	★			
SHOWDOWN	179			★	★		★	•			
SIMILARITY GROUPS	193	★		★	★					★	
SIMULTANEOUS RALLYTABLE	147			★	★		★	•	★	★	
SIMULTANEOUS ROUNDTABLE	169		★	★	★		★	•	★	★	
SINGLE ROUNDROBIN	159		★	★	★		★	•	★	★	
SINGLE ROUNDTABLE	170		★	★	★		★	•	★	★	
SNOWBALL	117	★		★	★		★	•			
TALKING CHIPS	199		★	★	★		•		★		
TEAM INTERVIEW	209			★	★				★	★	★
THINK-WRITE-ROUNDROBIN	160		★	★	★		★	★	★	★	
TIMED PAIR INTERVIEW	223			★	★		•	•	★	★	•
TIMED PAIR SHARE	217			★	★			•	★	★	★
TIMED ROUNDROBIN	160		★	★	★		★		★	★	
TIMED ROUNDTABLE	170		★	★	★		★	•	•	★	
TRAVELING HEADS TOGETHER	96			★	★	•	★	★	★		
TRAVELING PAIR SHARE	227	★		★	★				★	★	
TRAVELING RALLYQUIZ	136	★		★	★		★	•			

Structure Functions

59 Kagan Structures
INTRODUCTION

By Dr. Spencer Kagan

STRUCTURES ARE EMPOWERING. They transform teaching and learning. When I think of the power of structures, I think of the power of a well-placed lever. Given the proper lever, with little effort we can lift a huge load. Structures are like that. With a little effort we can dramatically increase academic achievement, reduce the achievement gap, improve social and ethnic relations, foster social skills and character, and reduce the incidence and severity of discipline problems. Structures are an educator's dream!

> "Give me a lever long enough and a fulcrum on which to place it, and I shall move the world."
> —Archimedes

Any thoughtful educator should question these claims. How can instructional strategies as simple as **RallyRobin** or **Timed Pair Share** transform teaching and learning? Although each structure fosters specific thinking skills and social skills, the structures all have something in common: They radically increase the amount of active engagement among students. And when students are actively engaged, learning is accelerated.

Let's examine how a simple structure transforms the amount of active engagement. Let's compare the amount of engagement in a traditional classroom with the amount in a classroom using Kagan Structures. After asking a question of the class, the traditional teacher calls on students one at a time to answer. To give a student 1 minute of active engagement—1 minute to verbalize his or her thinking in response to the teacher's question, it takes about 2 minutes. Why? First, the teacher has to ask the question, then the student answers the question, and then the teacher responds to the student's answer. The teacher talks twice for each time the student talks, so it takes about 2 minutes to give a student 1 minute of active verbalization. With approximately 30 students in the class, the best the teacher can do is give each student 1 minute of active engagement per hour!

In contrast, after asking the same question of the class, the teacher uses **RallyRobin** or **Timed Pair Share**, allowing students 2 minutes to interact. In 2 minutes every student in the class has had a minute of active engagement. Using Kagan Structures, the teacher accomplishes in 2 minutes what the traditional teacher would take an hour to accomplish; Kagan Structures produce 30 times as much active engagement!

RallyRobin and **Timed Pair Share** are just two examples of the many Kagan Structures in this book. They are alternatives to the ever-present traditional question and answer sessions. Structures multiply student engagement by unleashing the power of simultaneous student-to-student interaction. All students are engaged at once instead of one at a time. The structures in this book provide alternatives to traditional teaching that escalate student engagement for many different learning objectives, including brainstorming, guided practice, reviews, test preparation, information processing, higher-level thinking, and more. When we use Kagan Structures as a regular part of the way we teach, students' classroom experience is radically transformed. Instead of listening passively or being engaged rarely, full engagement becomes the daily norm. Kagan Structures actively engage all students!

> Why would we want to call on just one student when in the same amount of time we could call on all students?

If increasing active engagement were all structures did, it would be enough of a justification to begin teaching with structures. Why? Because students who are not engaged by the traditional classroom structure disengage from schooling. They tune out, fall behind, and when the gap becomes oppressive, drop out. Engagement is like a safety net for the classroom. It catches students who otherwise would fall through the cracks of our traditional educational system. When they are engaged, students learn so much more. The gap between the higher and lower achievers shrinks because the students who could opt to tune out are tuning in with great interest and excitement as they interact with partners, teammates, and classmates over the curriculum. The gap shrinks by engaging the disengaged and bringing the bottom up.

Full student engagement boosts student learning and decreases the achievement gap. But structures do so much more. Kagan Structures build social skills and transform social orientation by creating a more cooperative and caring classroom. When students compete for the teacher's attention, learning is a competition where students hope to beat their classmates so they can shine. When learning is independent, students learn that they are in it for themselves. In stark contrast in the classroom that uses Kagan Structures, students interact with each other. They share learning goals. They are on the same side. They hope for the success of their classmates and they help each other learn. Strangers become friends, and bullies become buddies. Discipline problems disappear, replaced by positive social skills and behaviors.

I have now trained teachers in almost 40 countries. In each country I observe classrooms. Worldwide the most common way teachers are structuring the interaction in their classroom is to ask a question and then call on a student who raises her/his hand. We need to look not at the faces of the students who are raising their hands, anxious to be called upon. We need to look instead at the faces and body language of those who are hiding, hoping not to be called upon. If we want to release the power of active engagement, we need to restructure our classrooms so every student has a voice.

After observing traditional classrooms, I always come away asking myself the same questions:

Why call on one, when we can call on all?

Why engage some, when we can engage everyone?

IN THIS BOOK

WHAT IS A KAGAN STRUCTURE?

Kagan Structures are the core of this book. Kagan Structures are interactive teaching and learning strategies designed to make learning more cooperative and engaging. Structures are a repeatable series of steps that describe how students interact with each other over the curriculum. They may be used with different subject matter and at different grade levels. For example, a primary teacher may use a RoundRobin in social studies to have students name community helpers; an elementary teacher may use a RoundRobin in science to have students review the steps of a math algorithm; and a secondary teacher may use a RoundRobin in language arts to share their written themes of a short story they just read. The steps of the structure are the same across the grade levels and across the curriculum. That's what makes structures so powerful. When you learn one new structure, you are empowered to use it to create engagement in so many different ways.

Kagan Structures were born of the theory and research on cooperative learning. Cooperative learning is one of the most extensively researched educational innovations of all times and study after study and meta-analysis after meta-analysis has confirmed its superior performance over traditional independent and competitive teaching methods for student learning. Teachers, schools, and districts using Kagan Structures have corroborated the research, reporting giant strides in educational attainment, increases in positive student behaviors, and decreases in discipline problems.

WHY SO MANY STRUCTURES?

There are so many strategies because there are so many things we need to accomplish in the classroom. Kagan Structures provide engaging alternatives to traditional teaching. Centerpiece, for example, is a way to brainstorm and share ideas in teams. Fan-N-Pick is a terrific team structure to review curriculum in a game-like fashion. RallyCoach is a pair problem solving structure—a wonderful alternative to traditional worksheet work. Each structure is good for reaching a different educational objective. Knowing which structure to use and when to use it is part of the art and science of teaching.

Another reason there are so many structures is because students crave novelty. If we do the same thing day in and day out, school becomes boring. It is a monotonous chore where every day looks like the last—different day, same structure. Motivation and learning are intricately intertwined. If students come to class and are engaged with different classmates in different ways, learning isn't stale. Class time is fresh and fun. Teachers who learn and use a variety of structures keep students motivated and excited to see how they will work with their classmates today. If variety of is the spice of life, structures are the spice of learning.

HOW ARE STRUCTURES ORGANIZED?

In this book, structures are organized alphabetically. However, related structures are nested within a structure. For example, in the structure RoundTable, you will find variations including Timed RoundTable, RoundTable Consensus, and Simultaneous RoundTable. Having similar structures nearby shows the relationship of the structure and makes it easy to find and learn like structures.

DEDICATION

This book is dedicated to a different vision for education. It is a vision where all students are actively engaged, every day. Where teachers have a rich array of structures to promote student interaction over the curriculum. It is a vision where students are much more motivated to learn because the classroom respects their natural desire to move, interact, and process information. Where students minds blossom because they understand and retain so much more of what they do and say than what they hear. This book is dedicated to a vision where students feel a sense of belonging in the classroom forged by positive daily interactions where they are known, liked, and respected by their classmates, teammates, and partners.

This book is dedicated to a vision of full student engagement. And this book is dedicated to you—the thoughtful educator who defiantly departs with tradition to embrace a revolutionary new way to teach in order to make this vision a reality for your students.

IN THIS BOOK Continued

HOW ARE STRUCTURES PRESENTED?

The main structures are presented in the same fashion: The structure has a short synopsis, making it easy to get the big picture at a glance. The synopsis is also helpful when searching for the right structure or for a quick refresher. There is a written description of the structure, painting a picture of what the structure looks like in action. Perhaps most helpful is the step-by-step directions for using the structure.

Please keep in mind that the steps were carefully crafted and each step is there for a reason. Structures are designed to incorporate research-based educational principles and each step has a purpose. If you leave out a step or two, you will be diminishing the effectiveness of the structure. For example, if you leave out a step, you may be leaving out the element that ensures equal participation for everyone. Or, you may be leaving out individual accountability which is crucial for boosting achievement for all. When we leave out important steps, we water down the structures with deleterious effects on student learning. Using the structures properly maximizes student benefits.

There are also practical tips for using the structure, developed over years of use. Ideas Across the Curriculum offer suggestions for how you might use the structure in mathematics, language arts, social studies, science, and other subjects. These ideas are intended to prime the pump for you to consider how you might use the structure in your own classroom. You know your curriculum best and we encourage you to brainstorm and jot down ideas for how you can integrate the structure into your own lesson plans.

Some structures also include blackline masters. Some blacklines are templates for you to use as you create your own activities using your own curriculum. Some blacklines are sample activities. These are not intended as activities for you to use with your students, but rather as example activities so you can see how you can design your own blacklines when using the structure. If you are looking for ready-to-use activities, Kagan offers many books across the grade levels and across the curriculum.

Related structures are presented in less detail than the main structures. They offer a description of the structure and brief step-by-step instructions.

Introduction

ALLRECORD ROUNDROBIN

Structure #1
ALLRECORD ROUNDROBIN

AllRecord RoundRobin adds independent writing to a team RoundRobin. After each student shares an idea orally with teammates, each student independently records the idea on his or her own paper, in his or her own words. Benefit: Each student retains a written record of what was shared.

STEPS
Getting Ready: *Each teammate needs a sheet of paper and a pen or pencil.*

Step 1
Teacher Assigns Topic

The teacher assigns a topic or question with multiple possible answers or provides a list of questions. For example, "*What are things we can do to conserve water?*"

Step 2
Students Respond

In teams, students each, in turn, respond orally while all students write each response on their own paper.

RELATED STRUCTURES

#2 AllRecord Consensus

AllRecord Consensus adds one feature to an AllRecord RoundRobin: consensus seeking. After each student shares an idea, teammates put their thumbs up if they agree. If they disagree or have doubt, they put a hand flat on the table. The team discusses the answer until they reach agreement or until a new, acceptable answer is proposed. Once the team reaches consensus, each student writes the answer in his or her own words on his or her own paper. The process is continued with each contribution: idea proposed, team consensus, and individual writing.

Step 1 Teacher Assigns Topic
The teacher assigns a topic or question with multiple possible answers or provides a list of questions.

Step 2 First Teammate Suggests Answer
One teammate suggests an answer.

Step 3 Seek Consensus
Students give a thumbs up to show agreement or a hand on the table if they disagree or have doubt. The team discusses the answer until they reach consensus.

Step 4 Students Record Answer
Once the team reaches consensus, each student writes the answer in his or her own words on his or her own paper.

Step 5 Repeat
The process is repeated with the next student suggesting an answer.

RECORDING SHEET
AllRecord RoundRobin

Instructions. Use this recording sheet to record everything shared in your team's RoundRobin.

I SHARED...

NAME

- _____
- _____
- _____
- _____
- _____

MY TEAMMATE SHARED...

NAME

- _____
- _____
- _____
- _____
- _____

MY TEAMMATE SHARED...

NAME

- _____
- _____
- _____
- _____
- _____

MY TEAMMATE SHARED...

NAME

- _____
- _____
- _____
- _____
- _____

Structure #3

CENTERPIECE

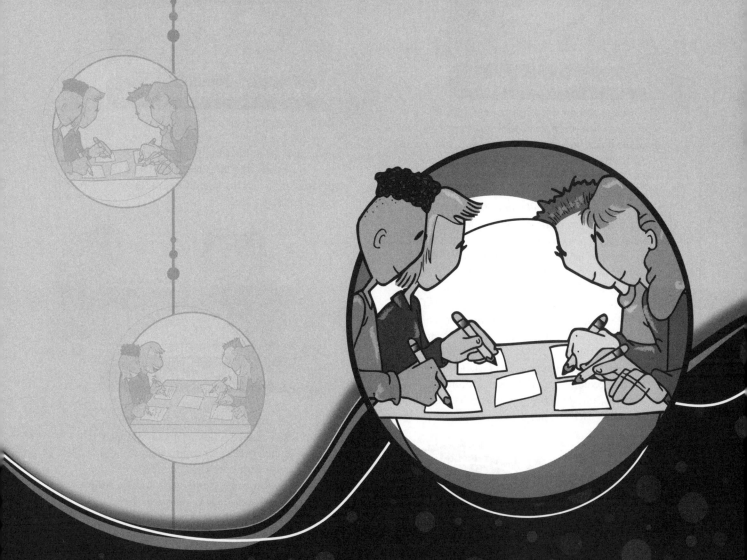

Structure #3
CENTERPIECE

Students brainstorm ideas and record their ideas on sheets of paper. To build team synergy, after recording each new idea, they trade their paper with the centerpiece.

STEPS **Getting Ready:** *Each teammate needs a sheet of paper. Plus, one sheet of paper, the "Centerpiece," is placed in the center of the team table.*

Step 1 — Teacher Assigns Topic

The teacher assigns a brainstorming topic or a problem with multiple possible answers. For example it can be a simple list such as, *"How many ways can you make $1 with coins?"* or *"What are some ways our class can raise funds to donate to the relief fund?"* The teacher encourages synergy as students use CenterPiece: *"You will brainstorm lots of ideas in your teams. As you read your teammates' ideas, see if you can piggyback on those ideas. Make them better. Or if they spur new ideas, record your new ideas. We don't care who came up with which idea, we just want the best ideas we can come up with as a team."*

Another way to do CenterPiece is for each paper to have a different, but related, topic. For example, the question might be, *"What can you find in each ecology?"* Each paper would be labeled with a different ecology: Desert, Ocean, Mountains, Grasslands, and Rain Forest. Students list items that are found in each ecology on their respective papers.

Step 2 — Students Generate Ideas

Each teammate writes an idea on his or her own sheet of paper. Then, the teammate exchanges his or her sheet of paper with the Centerpiece, the sheet in the center of the team table. Each student writes ideas at his or her own pace.

Step 3 — Students Synergize

Students scan the ideas teammates generated on the new Centerpiece sheet they receive. Students are encouraged to piggyback on teammate ideas, or to contribute new ideas. Students continue brainstorming items, each time recording them on the new Centerpiece they have taken, then trading their paper for another Centerpiece.

IDEAS Across the Curriculum

Mathematics

Students brainstorm…

- Word problems for a given equation
- Ways to equal 100
- Fractions in the real world
- Things that have a circular shape
- Draw acute/obtuse angles
- Draw symmetrical/asymmetrical shapes
- Uses of graphs

Language Arts

Students brainstorm…

- Characters in a book/play
- Words that rhyme with *eight*
- Possible settings for a story
- Nouns
- Adjectives describing a character
- Possible topic sentences for a paragraph
- Words that start with *s*
- Words that have the "ch" sound
- Rhyming words
- Metaphors
- Idioms

Social Studies

Students brainstorm…

- What would be different if…
- Events in the chapter/unit
- Historical figures in the era
- Landforms studied
- States/countries/oceans
- Facts about an event
- Community helpers
- Solutions to a social issue

Science

Students brainstorm…

- Possible outcomes of an experiment
- Hypotheses
- Vertebrates
- Constellations
- Exercises
- Bones/body parts
- Foods high in proteins/fats/calories
- Birds
- Ocean animals
- Elements
- Healthy snacks
- Items that use electricity
- Recyclable items
- Predators/prey
- Systems of the body

Teambuilding

Students brainstorm…

- Favorite TV shows
- Favorite songs
- Favorite things to do around town
- Things to do on a rainy day
- Qualities of a good friend/teammate
- Favorite places to go
- Random acts of kindness
- Things to bring to the beach
- Things to bring to the mountain
- Cartoons
- Cereals

CenterPiece

STORY ELEMENTS
CenterPiece

Instructions. List one thing you recall about the story and switch papers with the Centerpiece.

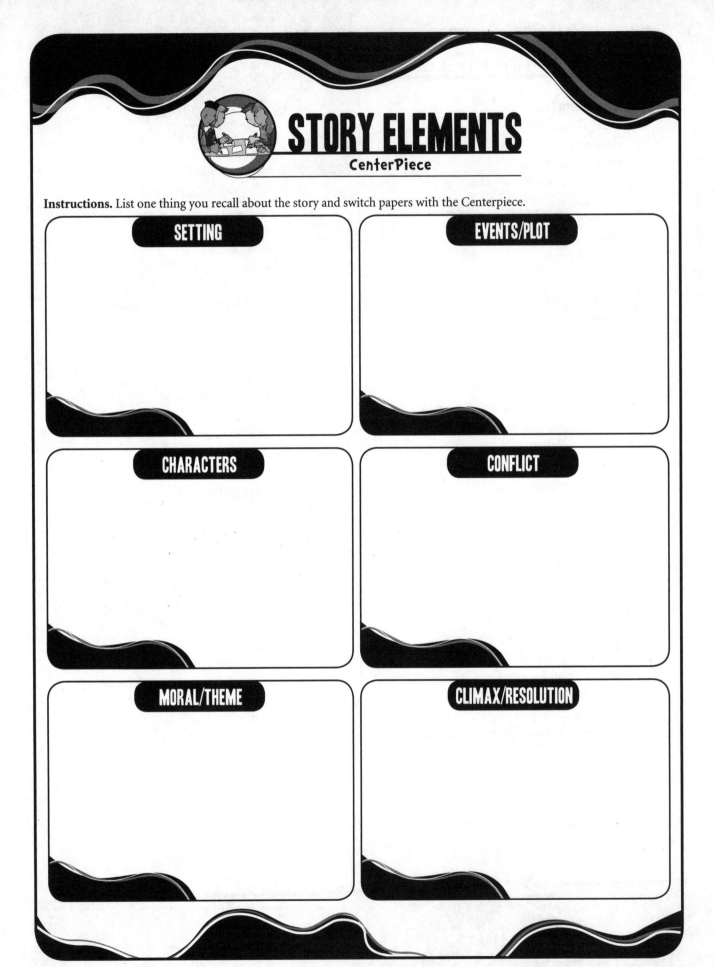

SETTING

EVENTS/PLOT

CHARACTERS

CONFLICT

MORAL/THEME

CLIMAX/RESOLUTION

REVOLUTION REVIEW
CenterPiece

Instructions. List one thing you recall learning about this revolution on this piece of paper. Then switch papers with the Centerpiece.

CAUSES

IMPORTANT PEOPLE

CONSEQUENCES

EVENTS

CONFLICTS

ANIMAL CLASSIFICATION
CenterPiece

Instructions. List one animal in its group, then switch papers with the Centerpiece.

MAMMALS

BIRDS

FISH

REPTILES

AMPHIBIANS

59 Kagan Structures
Kagan Publishing • 1 (800) 933-2667 • KaganOnline.com

Structure #4

FAN-N-PICK

FAN-N-PICK

Teammates rotate roles as they ask, answer, paraphrase, and praise, or coach each other.

FAN-N-PICK is a highly structured, but fun team process for responding to questions. Each team receives their own set of question or problem cards. The cards can have review questions about the chapter the class just read, they can be mastery-oriented problems or flashcards, or they can be open-ended thinking questions. Student #1 fans the deck of cards and holds the fan up to Student #2. Student #1 says, *"Pick a card, any card!"* Student #2 picks any card from the deck, reads the question to the team, and gives the team some Think Time.

For reading comprehension, it might sound like, *"What would be a good title for the story? Think of a good title for 5 seconds."* Then, Student #3 answers the question, *"I think 'The Woman Who Changed the World' is a good title."* Student #4 responds. If the question is a thinking question, Student #4 paraphrases and praises the response, *"Excellent title. It really captures the essence of the story."* If the question has a right or wrong response, Student #4 checks the answer and praises or tutors. *"Actually 'adumbrate' means to give a faint shadow or slight representation of, or to shade or overshadow. I remember it because the 'umbr' in the word is like umbrella, and umbrellas can give shade."* Teammates rotate roles for each new question.

Fan-N-Pick is terrific for turn taking, equal participation, and individual accountability. Students each have a role in the questioning process and the roles are rotated so that everyone plays each role.

DIFFERENTIATED INSTRUCTION

Different ability groups may be given different leveled questions. Students or teams can answer at the appropriate level of difficulty: some may be required to state their answers, others to draw their answers, and yet others to write their answers.

BENEFITS

Students...

...each play an important role.

...rotate roles so they perform each role.

...have fun as questions and reviews become game-like.

...are each accountable for participating.

Pick a card...
any card!

Student #1 Fans Cards

Student #1 holds the question cards in a fan and says, "*Pick a card, any card!*"

Step 2

Student #2 Picks a Card

Student #2 picks a card, reads the question aloud to the team, holds the card up so #3 can see the question for 5 seconds, then lays the card down. (For cards that have answers on the back, Student #2 passes the card to Student #4 to check for correctness.) "*What time is it if the little hand is between the two and three and the big hand is on the six?*"

Step 3

Student #3 Answers

Student #3 answers the question. "*It's two-thirty.*" For problem solving, have students think aloud as they write so teammates can hear their thinking process.

Step 4

Student #4 Responds

Student #4 responds to the answer.
- For right or wrong answers: Student #4 checks the answer and then either praises or tutors the student who answered. "*That's correct! You're a true genius.*" or "*I don't think that's correct; let's solve it again together.*"
- For higher-level thinking questions that have no right or wrong answer: Student #4 does not check for correctness, but praises the thinking that went into the answer and/or paraphrases. "*You gave three plausible reasons why the main character left home. I like the way you approached the question.*"

Step 5

Rotate Roles

Teammates rotate roles, one person clockwise for each new round.

Fan-N-Pick

STRUCTURE POWER

While the traditional teacher is asking questions of students one at a time, the teacher using Fan-N-Pick has a student in each team answering a question. Why would we want one student in the class answering a question if in the same amount of time we could have one student in each team answering? But Fan-N-Pick does much more than just increase engagement: Students learn to praise, augment, tutor, take turns, and enjoy learning. Fan-N-Pick is another structure that lends itself to easy differentiation: Students can play in different ability level teams with different content or different levels of questions.

TIPS

• **Model It.** Model Fan-N-Pick with one team before having teams play.

• **Mat.** Use the Fan-N-Pick mat provided. The mat lists the four roles so students each know their responsibilities. The mat is rotated for each question.

• **Role Cards.** Use the role cards provided. Role cards are rotated with each new question so that students and the teacher can see at a glance whose turn it is to perform each action.

• **Role Pyramid.** Create a pyramid with a square base and four faces. One role is written on each face. The pyramid is placed in the center of the team table. Students assume the role on the pyramid facing them. The pyramid is rotated with each new question.

• **Repeats?** Tell teams in advance whether the question card goes back in the stack or if it is removed, so the question is not repeated.

• **Student Questions.** Have students or teams create the questions cards.

• **Thumbs Up or Sideways.** If the student responsible for checking the answer doesn't know, he or she may ask teammates to indicate with thumbs up, if they agree, or thumbs sideways if they don't. Teammates must then tutor the student who did not know the answer.

• **If Students Can't Answer.** If none of the teammates knows the answer, all four teammates raise a hand to signal they have a Team Question. The teacher then consults with the team.

• **Answers.** For problems with right or wrong answers, it is helpful to provide the answers for students to self-check each problem. The answers may be on the back of each card, on the bottom of the card when students can cover the answer, or on a separate answer key.

Mathematics

Students answer questions about:
- Math facts
- Number identification
- Money
- Time
- Graphing questions
- Word problems

Language Arts

Students answer questions about:
- Spelling words
- Comprehension questions
- Parts of speech/punctuation
- Character
- Setting, plot
- Grammar

Social Studies

Students answer questions about:
- Community
- State
- Constitution
- Culture
- Geography
- Current events
- Chapter review

Science

Students answer questions about:
- Inventions
- Space
- Animals
- Chemical reactions
- Plants
- Ecosystems
- Matter
- Energy
- Animals
- Solar system

Music

Students answer questions about:
- Instruments
- Note names
- Musicians

Art

Students answer questions about:
- Styles of art
- Art tools
- Who's the artist?

Teambuilding

Students answer questions about:
- Personal questions
- Food
- Vacations
- Pets
- Hobbies
- Family
- TV shows

Second Language

Students answer questions about:
- House
- Clothes
- Animals
- Foods
- Community
- Grammar
- Careers
- Human body
- Weather
- Sports
- Transportation

Fan-N-Pick

VARIATION

- **Fan-N-Spin.** The team plays Fan-N-Pick with a random team selector spinner. After a question is read, the reader spins the spinner and the selected student answers. This keeps everyone thinking because anyone may be called on to answer at any point. The student to the left of the student who answered responds to the answer. For right or wrong answers, the student checks the answer. For thinking questions, the responding student either paraphrases and/or praises the answer.

RELATED STRUCTURES

#5 Dip-A-Strip

Dip-A-Strip is a hybrid structure, borrowing pieces from Fan-N-Pick and Sage-N-Scribe. Questions are written on strips instead of cards. It is easy to take an existing worksheet and cut it into strips. Each team receives a baggie with question strips. Student #1 "Dips for a strip" (pulls a question strip from the baggie), then reads it aloud and places it faceup in front of Student #2. Student #2 is the Sage and orally gives instructions to Student #3, the Scribe, to work out the problem (or record the answer) on a paper or response board. Student #4 checks the answer and leads the team in coaching, praising, or in a team celebration. Students rotate roles one clockwise for each new round. Play continues until all strips are used, or until the teacher calls time.

Step 1

Student # 1 Pulls a Strip

Student #1 dips for a strip and then reads it aloud and places it faceup in front of Student #2.

Step 2

Student # 2 Instructs

Student #2 is the Sage and orally gives instructions to Student #3, the Scribe, to work out the problem (or record the answer) on a paper or response board.

Step 3

Student # 4 Checks

Student #4 checks the answer and leads the team in coaching, praising, or in a team celebration.

Step 4

Students Rotate

Students rotate roles one clockwise for each new round. Play continues until all strips are used, or until the teacher calls time.

#6 Fan-N-Pick Partners

Fan-N-Pick can also be played in pairs. Partner A fans the cards and asks Partner B to *"Pick a card, any card."* Partner B picks a card, reads the question aloud, and allows 5 seconds of Think Time. Partner A answers the question. Partner B responds. For right/wrong answers, Partner B checks the answer and congratulates his or her partner if correct, or if incorrect, provides coaching. For open-ended questions, Partner B paraphrases the response, then praises it. Students trade roles for each new question. The advantage of playing in pairs is that students are more active throughout the process. There is less downtime. Playing in teams, however, creates greater variety and provides more resources for coaching and tutoring. For novelty, play Fan-N-Pick in teams and occasionally in pairs, too.

Partner A Fans Cards
Partner A holds question cards in a fan and says, *"Pick a card, any card!"*

Partner B Picks a Card
Partner B picks a card, reads the question aloud, and allows five seconds of Think Time.

Partner A Answers
Partner A answers the question.

Partner B Responds
Partner B responds to the answer:
- For right or wrong answers, Partner B checks and then either praises or tutors.
- For questions that have no right or wrong answer, Partner B does not check for correctness, but praises and then paraphrases the thinking that went into the answer.

Students Switch
Students switch roles for each new round.

FAN-N-PICK ROLE MAT

Fan-N-Pick

Instructions. Place this Fan-N-Pick Role Mat in the center of the team table so that one role is facing each teammate. For each new round of Fan-N-Pick, rotate the mat clockwise so that each teammate gets a new role.

1

Fan

Fan cards and say, *"Pick a card, any card!"*

2

Pick

Pick a card and read it aloud.

4

Respond

Check the answer or paraphrase and praise.

3

Answer

Answer the question or solve the problem.

Instructions. Use these Fan-N-Pick Role Cards to play Fan-N-Pick.

Fan cards and say, *"Pick a card, any card!"*

Fan

FOLD

#1 FAN

Pick a card and read it aloud.

Pick

FOLD

#2 PICK

Instructions. Use these Fan-N-Pick Role Cards to play Fan-N-Pick.

Answer the question or solve the problem.

Answer

#3 ANSWER

Check the answer or paraphrase and praise.

Respond

#4 RESPOND

ROLE PYRAMID
Fan-N-Pick

Instructions. Copy the four sides of this Role Pyramid onto construction paper. Tape the sides together onto the square below and then tape them together to form a pyramid.

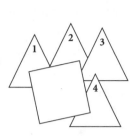

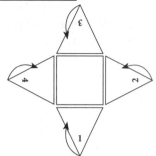

Fan-N-Pick
INSTRUCTIONS

1 STUDENT #1 FANS CARDS
Student #1 holds the question cards in a fan and says, "*Pick a card, any card!*"

2 STUDENT #2 PICKS A CARD
Student #2 picks a card, reads the question aloud to the team, holds the card up so that Student #3 can see the question for 5 seconds, and then lays the card down. (For cards that have answers on the back, Student #2 passes the card to Student #4 to check for correctness.) "*What time is it if the little hand is between the two and three and the big hand is on the six?*"

3 STUDENT #3 ANSWERS
Student #3 answers the question.
"*It's two-thirty.*"

4 STUDENT #4 RESPONDS
Student #4 responds to the answer.
- For right or wrong answers: Student #4 checks the answer and then either praises or tutors the student who answered. "*That's correct! You're a true genius.*" or "*I don't think that's correct; let's solve it again together.*"
- For higher-level thinking questions that have no right or wrong answer: Student #4 does not check for correctness, but praises the thinking that went into the answer and/or paraphrases. "*You gave three plausible reasons why the main character left home. I like the way you approached the question.*"

5 ROTATE ROLES
Teammates rotate roles, one person clockwise for each new round.

Instructions. Copy the four sides of this Role Pyramid onto construction paper. Tape the sides together onto the square and then tape them together to form a pyramid.

1

Fan

Fan cards and say,
"Pick a card, any card!"

Fan-N-Pick

Instructions. Copy the four sides of this Role Pyramid onto construction paper. Tape the sides together onto the square and then tape them together to form a pyramid.

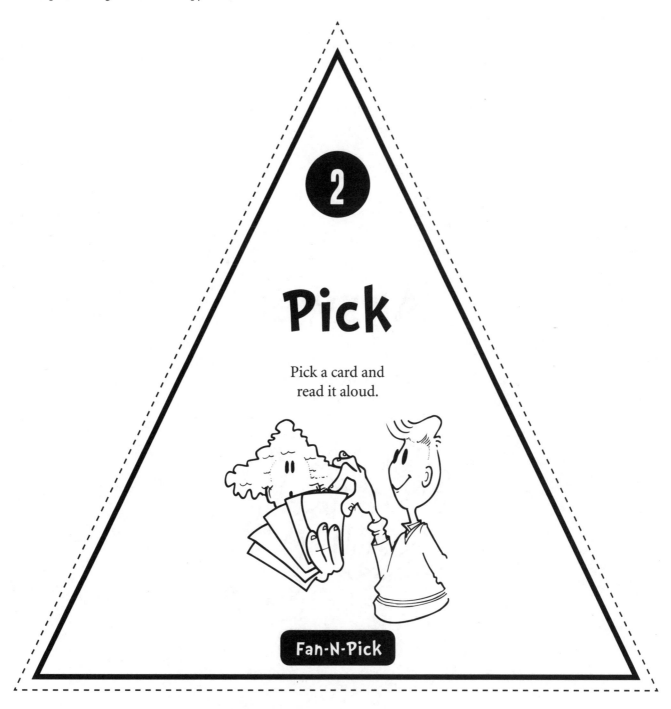

2

Pick

Pick a card and
read it aloud.

Fan-N-Pick

Instructions. Copy the four sides of this Role Pyramid onto construction paper. Tape the sides together onto the square and then tape them together to form a pyramid.

3

Answer

Answer the question or
solve the problem.

Fan-N-Pick

Instructions. Copy the four sides of this Role Pyramid onto construction paper. Tape the sides together onto the square and then tape them together to form a pyramid.

4

Respond

Check the answer or
paraphrase and praise.

Fan-N-Pick

CALCULATING AREA
Fan-N-Pick

Instructions. Cut out the Calculating Area cards and play Fan-N-Pick to solve the area of each rectangle.

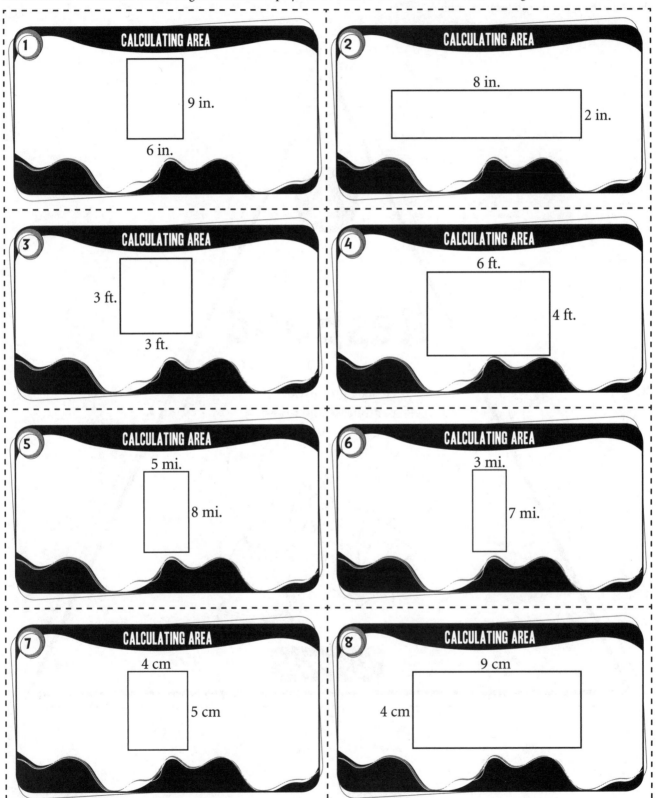

1 CALCULATING AREA

9 in.

6 in.

2 CALCULATING AREA

8 in.

2 in.

3 CALCULATING AREA

3 ft.

3 ft.

4 CALCULATING AREA

6 ft.

4 ft.

5 CALCULATING AREA

5 mi.

8 mi.

6 CALCULATING AREA

3 mi.

7 mi.

7 CALCULATING AREA

4 cm

5 cm

8 CALCULATING AREA

9 cm

4 cm

GETTING TO KNOW YOU
Fan-N-Pick

Instructions. Cut out the Getting to Know You cards and play Fan-N-Pick to answer the questions.

---

1 GETTING TO KNOW YOU

If you could go anywhere in the world for one week, where would you go? What would you do?

---

2 GETTING TO KNOW YOU

What is one of the best gifts you ever received?

---

3 GETTING TO KNOW YOU

What is one of the things you just couldn't live without and why?

---

4 GETTING TO KNOW YOU

What is one of the scariest things that ever happened to you, and why was it scary?

---

5 GETTING TO KNOW YOU

If you could win a prize, what would it be?

---

6 GETTING TO KNOW YOU

How would you describe your perfect day?

---

7 GETTING TO KNOW YOU

What is one of your favorite movies, books, or TV shows (pick one)? Describe why.

---

8 GETTING TO KNOW YOU

What would you do with 1 million dollars?

CARD TEMPLATE
Fan-N-Pick

Instructions. Use this blank Card Template to create your own Fan-N-Pick cards.

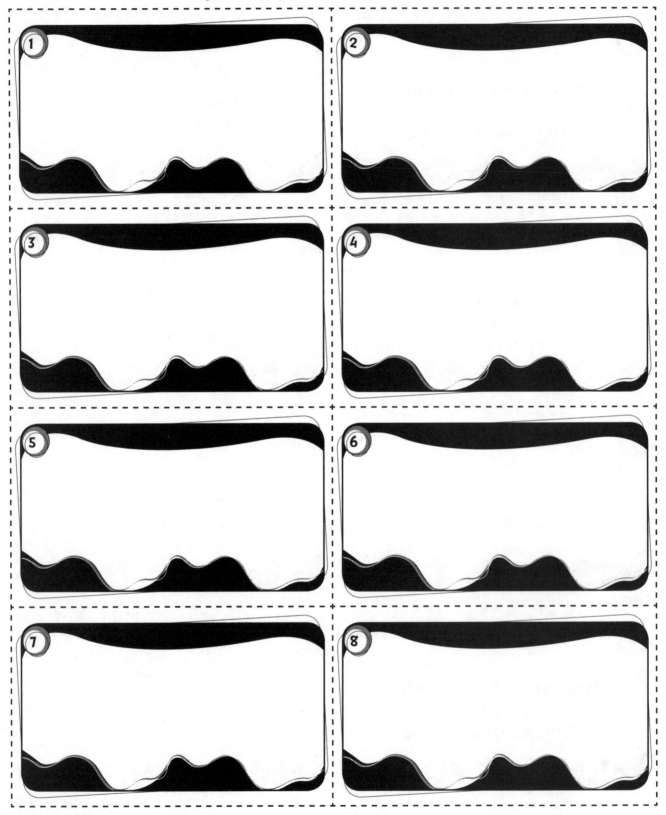

EQUIVALENCY
Fan-N-Pick

Instructions. Cut out each Equivalency card along the dotted line. Fold each card along the solid line so you have the question on one side and the answer on the other. Cards may be glued or taped to keep questions and answers on opposite sides.

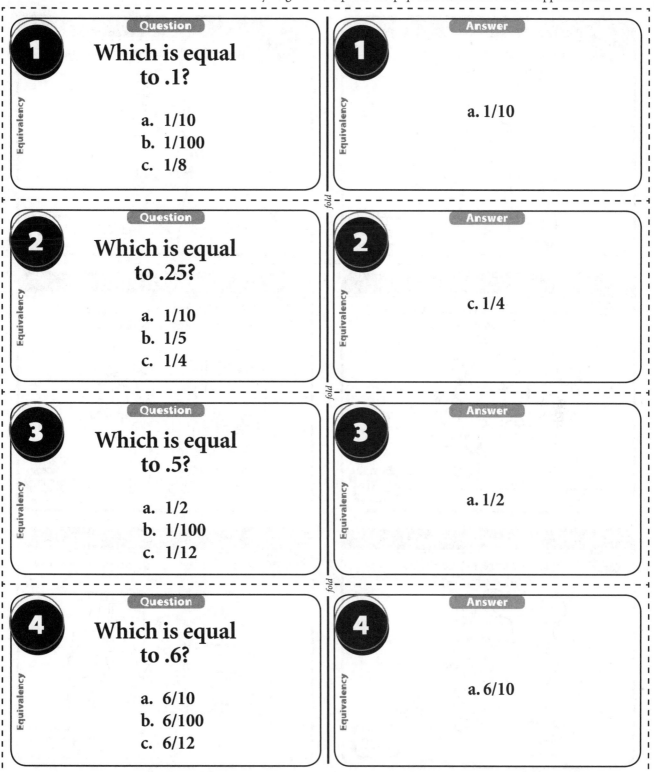

1 | **Question**
Which is equal to .1?

a. 1/10
b. 1/100
c. 1/8

1 | **Answer**

a. 1/10

2 | **Question**
Which is equal to .25?

a. 1/10
b. 1/5
c. 1/4

2 | **Answer**

c. 1/4

3 | **Question**
Which is equal to .5?

a. 1/2
b. 1/100
c. 1/12

3 | **Answer**

a. 1/2

4 | **Question**
Which is equal to .6?

a. 6/10
b. 6/100
c. 6/12

4 | **Answer**

a. 6/10

SOURCE: Stites, R. & Pfannenstiel, A. *Cooperative Math Grades 3–5*. San Clemente, CA: Kagan Publishing.

59 Kagan Structures
Kagan Publishing • 1 (800) 933-2667 • KaganOnline.com

À QUELLE HEURE?
(AT WHAT TIME?)
Fan-N-Pick

Instructions: Copy a set of *À quelle heure?* cards for each team. Cut out each card along the dotted line. Give each team a set of cards so that they can ask teammates at what time the person performs the activity on the card.

1 Fan-N-Pick
À quelle heure est-ce qu'il joue au basketball?

2:00

2 Fan-N-Pick
À quelle heure est-ce qu'elle danse?

4:30

3 Fan-N-Pick
À quelle heure est-ce qu'ils font leurs devoirs?

6:30

4 Fan-N-Pick
À quelle heure est-ce qu'elles regardent la télévision?

8:00

5 Fan-N-Pick
À quelle heure est-ce qu'ils jouent au hockey?

5:30

6 Fan-N-Pick
À quelle heure est-ce qu'il se lève?

7:00

SOURCE: Jozin, C. *Cooperative Learning & French*. San Clemente, CA: Kagan Publishing.

Structure #7

FLASHCARD STAR

Structure #7
FLASHCARD STAR

Students circulate in the room quizzing new partners, hoping to retire cards from their practice deck.

STEPS

Getting Ready: *The teacher provides students with flashcards on items they don't know, or students create the cards on missed items following a pre-test. Cards have a question on the front and an answer on the back. Each student needs a marker or something to write with.*

Step 1 · Students Pair Up

Students collect a pen or marker and five flashcards, stand up, put a hand up, and pair up.

Step 2 · Partners Trade Cards

Students trade flashcards with their partners, so partners can quiz each other using the cards students need to master.

Step 3 · Partner A Quizzes Partner B

Partner A selects one flashcard and quizzes Partner B. For example, Partner A shows the name of a country and asks, *"What is the capital?"*

Step 4 · Partner B Answers

Partner B attempts to answer.

59 Kagan Structures
Kagan Publishing • 1 (800) 933-2667 • KaganOnline.com

TIPS

· Coaching Tips. Instruct the class how to be a good coach and to offer helpful tips.

· Show the Card. During quizzing, it is helpful for partners to show the question or problem as well as read it. This provides visual and auditory cues. (Spelling word flashcards are an exception.) The same is true for the answer. Partners should say and show the correct answer when possible.

· Fold-N-Flash Cards. The question and answer are written on the same side of the card. The card is folded in half so the answer is behind the question. To reveal the answer, the card is unfolded. Fold-N-Flash cards allow students to see the question and answer at the same time, making a stronger visual connection.

· Challenge Cards. Because some students will finish more quickly than others, the teacher provides bonus cards to draw from.

Step
5
Partner A Checks Answer

If Partner B responds correctly, Partner A congratulates Partner B and puts a star on the front of the card. If the answer is not correct, Partner A states the correct answer and provides coaching or a tip. For example, *"Beijing is the capital of China. I think 'Being' in the capital of China."*

Step
6
A Quizzes B on Next Card

Partner A selects a second flashcard and quizzes Partner B. Partner B stars the card if correct or provides coaching or a tip. Partners only quiz each other on two cards, so they are frequently quizzing new partners for variety and movement.

Step
7
Switch Roles

Partners switch roles and Partner B quizzes Partner A on two cards.

Step
8
New Partners

Partners thank each other, each put a hand up, and seek new partners. When a card receives two stars, it is retired from the deck. When all five cards are retired, the student returns to his or her desk to gather five more cards.

Flashcard Star

FLASHCARD TEMPLATE
Flashcard Star

Instructions. Use this Flashcard Template to make your own flashcards for Flashcard Star. Fill in a star when the answer is correct.

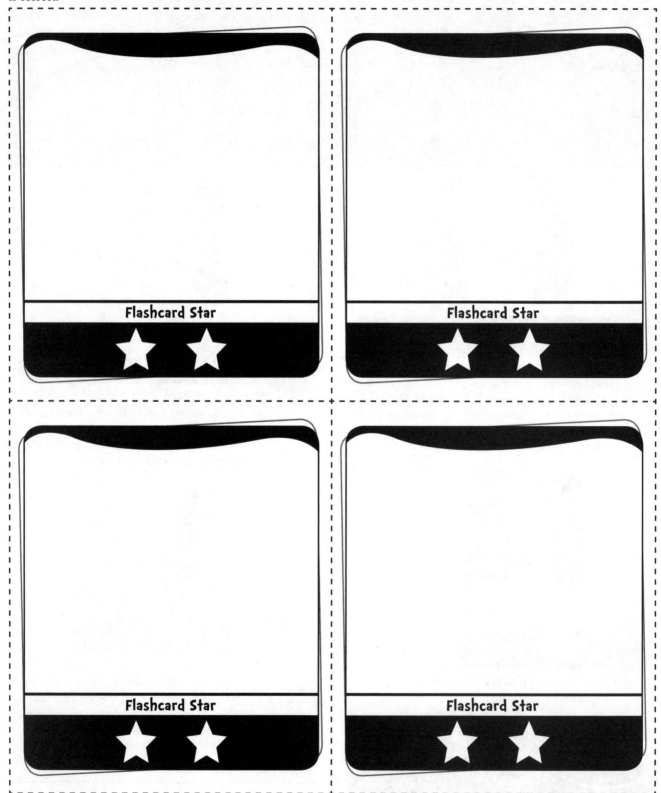

Flashcard Star

Flashcard Star

Flashcard Star

Flashcard Star

59 Kagan Structures
Kagan Publishing • 1 (800) 933-2667 • KaganOnline.com

Structure #8

IDEA ROUNDUP!

Structure #8

IDEA ROUNDUP!

Students repeatedly pair up to "RoundUp" ideas from different partners.

STEPS

Getting Ready

Students each have a recording sheet or something to write on and something to write with.

Step 1 — Teacher Announces Topic

The teacher announces the topic and provides student Think Time. For example, *"What are some real-world examples of when you may need to know fractions?"* Or, *"What are the events from the story?"*

Step 2 — StandUp–HandUp–PairUp

Students stand up, put a hand up, and pair up with a classmate. After pairing, students lower their hands, indicating they have a partner.

Step 3 — Partner A Shares Idea

Partner A shares one idea with Partner B.

Step 4 Partner B Records Idea

Partner B records the idea on his or her sheet or response board. Partner B thanks Partner A. *"Thanks for the great idea!"*

Step 5 Switch Roles

Partner B shares one idea with Partner A. Partner A records the idea and thanks Partner B.

Step 6 Repeat with New Partners

Students high five their partners and keep a hand up to find a new partner to repeat the process until time is called.

Optional

Students may use RoundRobin in their teams to share ideas they have gathered during Idea RoundUp!

Idea RoundUp!

IDEA ROUNDUP! SHEET
Idea RoundUp!

Instructions. Use this sheet to record ideas you collect from classmates during Idea RoundUp!

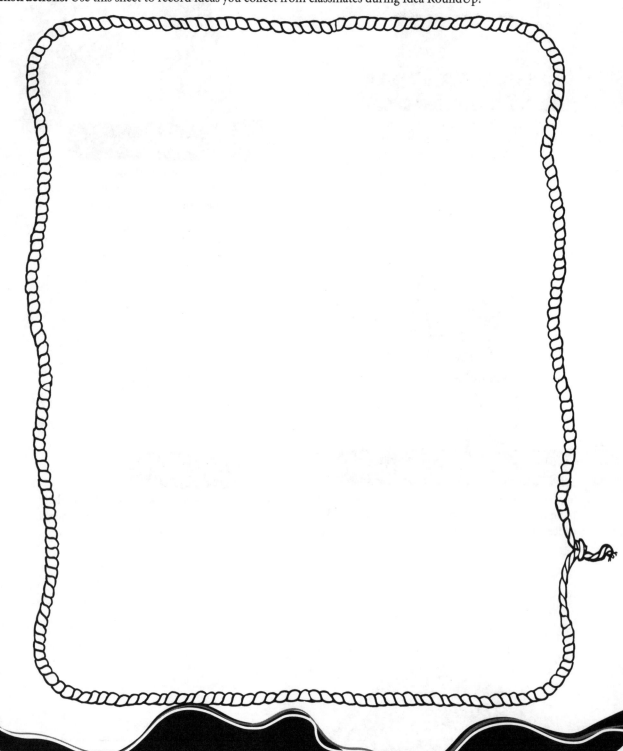

Structure #9

INSIDE-OUTSIDE CIRCLE

INSIDE-OUTSIDE CIRCLE

Students rotate in concentric circles to face new partners for sharing, quizzing, or problem solving.

FOR INSIDE-OUTSIDE CIRCLE, students form two concentric circles. Both circles have the same number of students. Students in the inside circle each face out, toward a student in the outside circle. There are two ways to structure Inside-Outside Circle: either teacher questions or question cards. With teacher oral questions, the teacher announces a topic or question, and students share with their partners. The share time can be an open-ended pair discussion, a Pair Share, or a Timed Pair Share so that each partner gets an equal time to share. With the question card format, pairs interact using question or problem cards. In this method, students each have a card and they use their cards to quiz a partner. After pairs have interacted, the teacher tells students to trade cards and then rotate so that they are facing a new partner to quiz.

Inside-Outside Circle is an energizing structure for having students quiz each other, share information, or share with classmates projects, writing, book reports, or other creative works.

DIFFERENTIATED INSTRUCTION

Two Inside-Outside Circles may be formed in the classroom, each with different difficulty leveled question cards and/or different content.

- For different difficulty level, one circle may have multiple-choice questions, whereas the other circle may have free recall questions.
- Students with special needs may be assigned a buddy and rotate with that buddy, who can offer support.

BENEFITS

Students...

...problem solve or share with many partners.

...hear multiple perspectives.

...repeatedly quiz classmates.

...are energized through movement.

...create novelty and maintain attention with each new partner.

Getting Ready: *The teacher prepares questions or problems, or the teacher or students prepare question cards, one per student. Students form A-B pairs.*

Step 1
Form the Outside Circle

Partner A from each pair moves to form one large circle in the class, facing in. "*Partner A's, please form a large circle in the open area of the classroom. B's watch where your partner goes.*"

Step 2
Form the Inside Circle

Partner B's find and face their partners. The class now stands in two concentric circles. "*Partner B's, please find and face your partners.*"

Step 3
Inside Circle Asks Question; Outside Circle Responds

Question Cards: Inside Circle students ask a question from their question card; Outside Circle students answer. Inside Circle students praise or coach.

Teacher Questions: The teacher asks a question and asks the Inside Circle students, Outside Circle students, or both (Timed Pair Share) to share with their partners. "*What did you do this weekend? Everyone think. Inside Circle students please share for 30 seconds.*"

continued

Inside-Outside Circle

Step 4 — Partners Switch Roles

Outside Circle students ask, listen, and then praise or coach. "*Outside Circle students, it's your turn to share for 30 seconds.*"

Step 5 — Partners Trade Cards

When using question cards, partners trade cards. To indicate they are ready to rotate, the Inside Circle students turn and face the center of the circle.

<table>
<tr>
<td>

Step 6 Rotate Partners

Students face their partners, then turn to touch right shoulders. Either the Inside Circle students or the Outside Circle students rotate to a new partner. The teacher may call rotation numbers: "*Face your partner. Turn sideways to touch right shoulders. Inside circle, rotate three students ahead.*" The class may do a "choral count" as they rotate.

</td>
<td>

Repeat:

Students rotate and quiz many times to discuss or solve problems with different partners.

</td>
</tr>
</table>

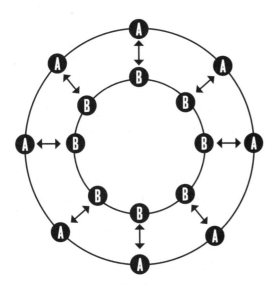

Interact in Pairs

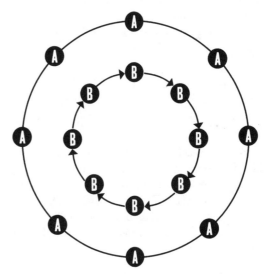

Inner Circle Rotates

Inside-Outside Circle

STRUCTURE POWER

Like many Kagan Structures, Inside-Outside Circle is brain-friendly: There is safety because students are answering to one supportive partner, not in front of the whole class. More oxygen and glucose flow to the brain because students are moving. Brains light up during social interaction. As students praise each other for correct answers, high emotion cements learning in memory. Feedback follows each answer. There is novelty—students rotate to new partners. And the whole experience is an episode, linking the content to episodic memory. When we teach using structures, we are teaching in ways our students' brains best learn!

TIPS

• **Small Steps.** Provide oral instructions to students at each step, so students know exactly what to do.

• **Practice Rotating.** Students may get hung up on how to rotate. Practice rotating a number of times before using questions, so students know how to rotate. Rotate only one circle at a time.

• **Extra Student.** If your class does not break evenly into pairs, have two students become "twins." Twins rotate together and take turns asking and answering questions.

• **Flashcards.** Have each student make up one question on a flashcard. Students ask each other their questions and switch cards before each rotation. With each rotation, students get new partner and a new question. The teacher can supply the flashcards, or act as a quality control filter by collecting and correcting the cards before they are used.

• **Student Discussion Questions.** Let students come up with questions to ask classmates. Put the questions in a hat and draw out one question each time the circle rotates.

• **Around the Perimeter.** Form circles around the perimeter of the classroom.

• **Play Outside.** If it is a nice day, bring the class outside to enjoy Inside-Outside Circle.

• **Vary Rotating.** To spice up rotating, vary the number of positions advanced, the circle that rotates, and the direction of rotation.

• **Choral Counting.** Have the class count aloud the number of positions they are moving so everyone knows when to stop. "*One, two, THREE!*"

• **Visual Signal.** Use a visual cue to know when students are ready to continue. For example, when finished with their question, students can stand back to back, side to side, or raise a hand.

• **Seated Circles.** Little ones may sit in circles on the floor. Only one circle stands to rotate. Chalk marks or carpet patches indicate where to stand or sit.

• **Random Teams.** Inside-Outside Circle can be used to form random teams: After several rotations, the teacher asks two adjacent pairs to step out of the circle and to sit down as a team of four. This creates a gap in the circle. The teacher then has the pairs at each end of the gap move forward, meet, and leave the circle to sit down as a team. The process continues Virginia Wheel–style to form the remaining teams.

IDEAS Across the Curriculum

Mathematics

Partners quiz each other on...

- Multiplication facts
- Rounding numbers
- Identifying shapes in a pattern
- Missing number in a problem
- Addition
- Solving for x
- Estimating answer
- Telling time
- Solving money problems
- Multiplying fractions
- Adding decimals
- Long division

Language Arts

Partners discuss or share...

- Story elements
- Prewriting questions
- Interpretations of pictures, charts, and tables
- Topic speaking

Partners quiz each other on...

- Contractions
- Spelling words
- Vocabulary words
- Reading comprehension
- Grammar
- Test prep

Social Studies

Partners discuss or share...

- Events
- Impact of inventions
- Most significant historical events that changed the world
- Country like to visit and why
- Events in history
- Drawbacks of a political system

Science

Partners discuss or share...

- How to protect endangered species
- Depletion of rain forest
- Recycling

Partners quiz each other on...

- Elements
- Cell parts
- Bones
- Organ functions
- Solar system facts

Classbuilding

Partners discuss or share...

- Show and tell
- What do you like to do alone, with others
- Person who had biggest impact on you
- Favorite singer
- Describe your family

Inside-Outside Circle

VARIATION

- **Pair Inside-Outside Circle.** Have students rotate in pairs and discuss in groups of four. A typical sequence might be, (1) the teacher asks a question, (2) the inside-circle pair discusses the question while the outside-circle pair discusses the question, and (3) the pairs compare their answers.

RELATED STRUCTURE

#10 Rotating Lines

Rotating Lines is very similar to Inside-Outside Circle. The big difference is students standing in facing lines instead of concentric circles. Lines are easier for younger students, work well with smaller groups, and may work better based on your room configuration.

Form Lines

Partner A's line up. Partner B's line up in a facing line.

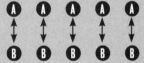

Teacher Asks Question

The teacher asks the class a question and states who will begin the Timed Pair Share. For example, "*What are you thankful for? Partner A share for 30 seconds.*"

Timed Pair Share

Both partners share for their allotted time and respond to their partner.

Rotate Lines

Have one line take a step forward so that students are facing a new partner for the next round of sharing. "*Partner A's, take a step forward to face the next partner in the other line.*"

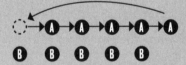

The first person in line is no longer facing a partner. That student walks to the end of the line to face the last student in the other line. Now, everyone is facing a new partner.

Repeat

The teacher asks the next question, and students interact with their new partners.

Note:

Like Inside-Oustide Circle, Rotating Lines can be structured in two ways: teacher questions or question cards. With question cards, partners quiz each other using the card, then trade cards before they rotate.

Instructions. Cut out the Greek Roots, Prefixes, and Suffixes cards and use them to quiz a partner in Inside-Outside Circle.

---

① GREEK ROOTS, PREFIXES, AND SUFFIXES

QUESTION: What is the meaning? Provide examples.

a-, an-

---

① GREEK ROOTS, PREFIXES, AND SUFFIXES

ANSWER:

Meaning: without
Examples: <u>a</u>moral, <u>a</u>typical, <u>an</u>onymous

---

② GREEK ROOTS, PREFIXES, AND SUFFIXES

QUESTION: What is the meaning? Provide examples.

-anthrop-

---

② GREEK ROOTS, PREFIXES, AND SUFFIXES

ANSWER:

Meaning: human
Examples: <u>anthrop</u>ic , phil<u>anthrop</u>y, <u>anthrop</u>omorphic, <u>anthrop</u>ology

---

③ GREEK ROOTS, PREFIXES, AND SUFFIXES

QUESTION: What is the meaning? Provide examples.

anti-, ant-

---

③ GREEK ROOTS, PREFIXES, AND SUFFIXES

ANSWER:

Meaning: opposite; against
Examples: <u>anti</u>crime, <u>anti</u>pollution, <u>ant</u>acid

---

④ GREEK ROOTS, PREFIXES, AND SUFFIXES

QUESTION: What is the meaning? Provide examples.

auto-

---

④ GREEK ROOTS, PREFIXES, AND SUFFIXES

ANSWER:

Meaning: self, same
Examples: <u>auto</u>biography, <u>auto</u>mobile, <u>auto</u>matic

---

GREEK ROOTS, PREFIXES, AND SUFFIXES
Inside-Outside Circle

Instructions. Cut out the Greek Roots, Prefixes, and Suffixes cards and use them to quiz a partner in Inside-Outside Circle.

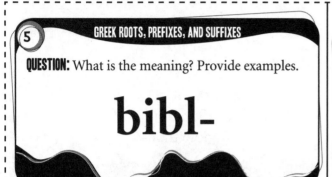

5 GREEK ROOTS, PREFIXES, AND SUFFIXES

QUESTION: What is the meaning? Provide examples.

bibl-

5 GREEK ROOTS, PREFIXES, AND SUFFIXES

ANSWER:

Meaning: book
Examples: bibliography, bible

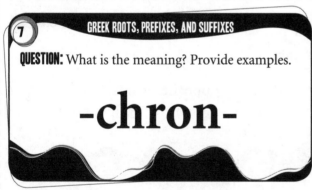

6 GREEK ROOTS, PREFIXES, AND SUFFIXES

QUESTION: What is the meaning? Provide examples.

bio-, bi-

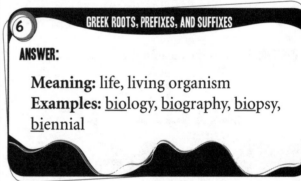

6 GREEK ROOTS, PREFIXES, AND SUFFIXES

ANSWER:

Meaning: life, living organism
Examples: biology, biography, biopsy, biennial

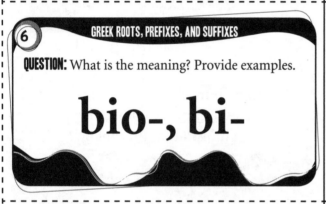

7 GREEK ROOTS, PREFIXES, AND SUFFIXES

QUESTION: What is the meaning? Provide examples.

-chron-

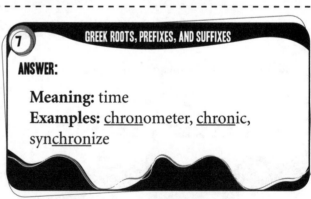

7 GREEK ROOTS, PREFIXES, AND SUFFIXES

ANSWER:

Meaning: time
Examples: chronometer, chronic, synchronize

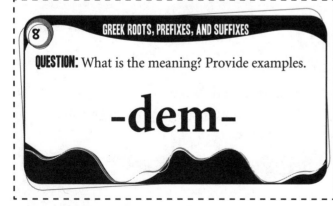

8 GREEK ROOTS, PREFIXES, AND SUFFIXES

QUESTION: What is the meaning? Provide examples.

-dem-

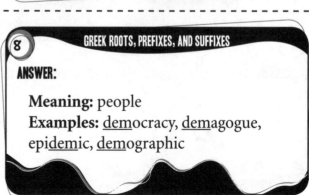

8 GREEK ROOTS, PREFIXES, AND SUFFIXES

ANSWER:

Meaning: people
Examples: democracy, demagogue, epidemic, demographic

59 Kagan Structures
Kagan Publishing • 1 (800) 933-2667 • KaganOnline.com

Instructions. Cut out the Greek Roots, Prefixes, and Suffixes cards and use them to quiz a partner in Inside-Outside Circle.

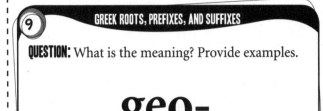

9 GREEK ROOTS, PREFIXES, AND SUFFIXES

QUESTION: What is the meaning? Provide examples.

geo-

9 GREEK ROOTS, PREFIXES, AND SUFFIXES

ANSWER:

Meaning: Earth; geography
Examples: geography, geology, geopolitics

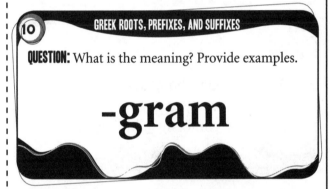

10 GREEK ROOTS, PREFIXES, AND SUFFIXES

QUESTION: What is the meaning? Provide examples.

-gram

10 GREEK ROOTS, PREFIXES, AND SUFFIXES

ANSWER:

Meaning: written or drawn, a record
Examples: cardiogram, telegram, seismogram

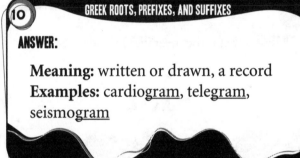

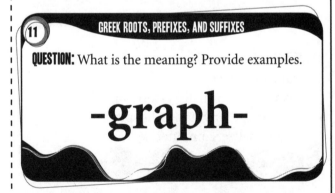

11 GREEK ROOTS, PREFIXES, AND SUFFIXES

QUESTION: What is the meaning? Provide examples.

-graph-

11 GREEK ROOTS, PREFIXES, AND SUFFIXES

ANSWER:

Meaning: written or drawn; an instrument for writing, drawing, or recording
Examples: photograph, graphical, phonograph, seismograph

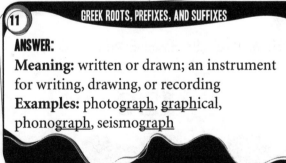

12 GREEK ROOTS, PREFIXES, AND SUFFIXES

QUESTION: What is the meaning? Provide examples.

hyper-

12 GREEK ROOTS, PREFIXES, AND SUFFIXES

ANSWER:

Meaning: above, excessively
Examples: hyperactive, hyperbole, hypersensitive

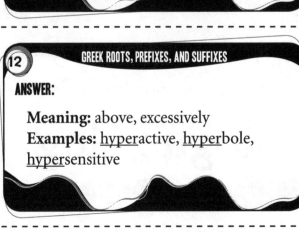

GREEK ROOTS, PREFIXES, AND SUFFIXES

Inside-Outside Circle

Instructions. Cut out the Greek Roots, Prefixes, and Suffixes cards and use them to quiz a partner in Inside-Outside Circle.

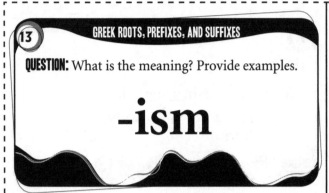

13 GREEK ROOTS, PREFIXES, AND SUFFIXES

QUESTION: What is the meaning? Provide examples.

-ism

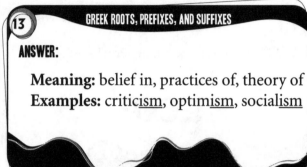

13 GREEK ROOTS, PREFIXES, AND SUFFIXES

ANSWER:

Meaning: belief in, practices of, theory of
Examples: critic<u>ism</u>, optim<u>ism</u>, social<u>ism</u>

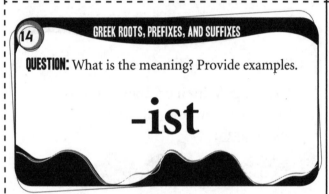

14 GREEK ROOTS, PREFIXES, AND SUFFIXES

QUESTION: What is the meaning? Provide examples.

-ist

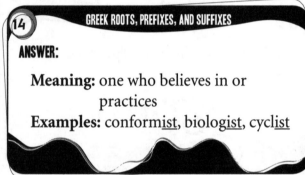

14 GREEK ROOTS, PREFIXES, AND SUFFIXES

ANSWER:

Meaning: one who believes in or practices
Examples: conform<u>ist</u>, biolog<u>ist</u>, cycl<u>ist</u>

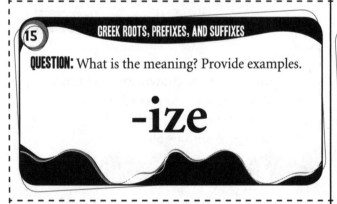

15 GREEK ROOTS, PREFIXES, AND SUFFIXES

QUESTION: What is the meaning? Provide examples.

-ize

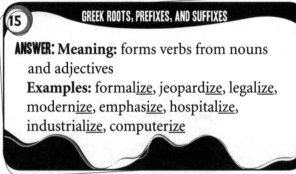

15 GREEK ROOTS, PREFIXES, AND SUFFIXES

ANSWER: Meaning: forms verbs from nouns and adjectives
Examples: formal<u>ize</u>, jeopard<u>ize</u>, legal<u>ize</u>, modern<u>ize</u>, emphas<u>ize</u>, hospital<u>ize</u>, industrial<u>ize</u>, computer<u>ize</u>

16 GREEK ROOTS, PREFIXES, AND SUFFIXES

QUESTION: What is the meaning? Provide examples.

-logue, -log

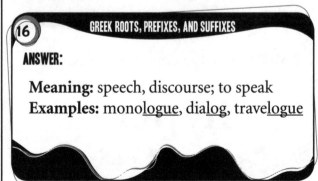

16 GREEK ROOTS, PREFIXES, AND SUFFIXES

ANSWER:

Meaning: speech, discourse; to speak
Examples: mono<u>logue</u>, dia<u>log</u>, trave<u>logue</u>

GREEK ROOTS, PREFIXES, AND SUFFIXES

Instructions. Cut out the Greek Roots, Prefixes, and Suffixes cards and use them to quiz a partner in Inside-Outside Circle.

---

(17) GREEK ROOTS, PREFIXES, AND SUFFIXES

QUESTION: What is the meaning? Provide examples.

-logy

---

(17) GREEK ROOTS, PREFIXES, AND SUFFIXES

ANSWER: Meaning: discourse, expression; science, theory, study
Examples: phraseo<u>logy</u>, bio<u>logy</u>, dermato<u>logy</u>

---

(18) GREEK ROOTS, PREFIXES, AND SUFFIXES

QUESTION: What is the meaning? Provide examples.

-meter, -metry

---

(18) GREEK ROOTS, PREFIXES, AND SUFFIXES

ANSWER:

Meaning: measurement
Examples: spectro<u>meter</u>, geo<u>metry</u>, kilo<u>meter</u>, para<u>meter</u>, peri<u>meter</u>

---

(19) GREEK ROOTS, PREFIXES, AND SUFFIXES

QUESTION: What is the meaning? Provide examples.

-micro-

---

(19) GREEK ROOTS, PREFIXES, AND SUFFIXES

ANSWER:

Meaning: small
Examples: <u>micro</u>cosm, <u>micro</u>chip, <u>micro</u>scope, sub<u>micro</u>scopic

---

(20) GREEK ROOTS, PREFIXES, AND SUFFIXES

QUESTION: What is the meaning? Provide examples.

mono-

---

(20) GREEK ROOTS, PREFIXES, AND SUFFIXES

ANSWER:

Meaning: one, single, alone
Examples: <u>mono</u>rail, <u>mono</u>syllable, <u>mono</u>cle

---

Instructions. Cut out the Greek Roots, Prefixes, and Suffixes cards and use them to quiz a partner in Inside-Outside Circle.

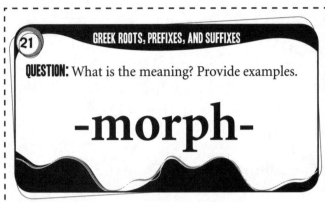

21 GREEK ROOTS, PREFIXES, AND SUFFIXES

QUESTION: What is the meaning? Provide examples.

-morph-

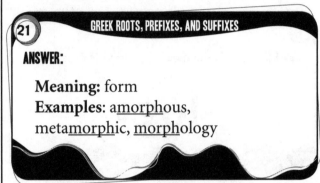

21 GREEK ROOTS, PREFIXES, AND SUFFIXES

ANSWER:

Meaning: form
Examples: amorphous, metamorphic, morphology

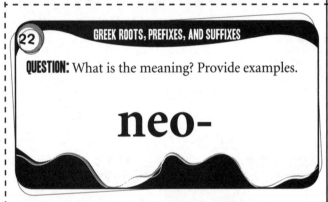

22 GREEK ROOTS, PREFIXES, AND SUFFIXES

QUESTION: What is the meaning? Provide examples.

neo-

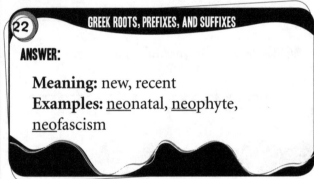

22 GREEK ROOTS, PREFIXES, AND SUFFIXES

ANSWER:

Meaning: new, recent
Examples: neonatal, neophyte, neofascism

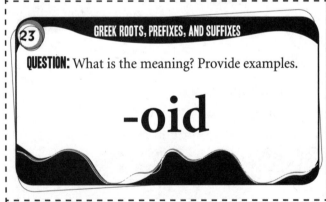

23 GREEK ROOTS, PREFIXES, AND SUFFIXES

QUESTION: What is the meaning? Provide examples.

-oid

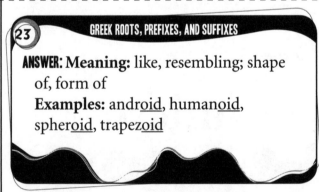

23 GREEK ROOTS, PREFIXES, AND SUFFIXES

ANSWER: Meaning: like, resembling; shape of, form of
Examples: android, humanoid, spheroid, trapezoid

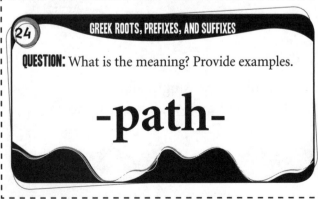

24 GREEK ROOTS, PREFIXES, AND SUFFIXES

QUESTION: What is the meaning? Provide examples.

-path-

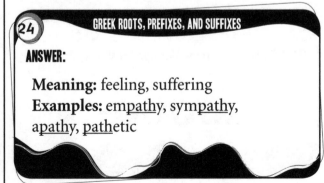

24 GREEK ROOTS, PREFIXES, AND SUFFIXES

ANSWER:

Meaning: feeling, suffering
Examples: empathy, sympathy, apathy, pathetic

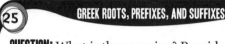

GREEK ROOTS, PREFIXES, AND SUFFIXES

Inside-Outside Circle

Instructions. Cut out the Greek Roots, Prefixes, and Suffixes cards and use them to quiz a partner in Inside-Outside Circle.

---

25 GREEK ROOTS, PREFIXES, AND SUFFIXES

QUESTION: What is the meaning? Provide examples.

ped-

---

25 GREEK ROOTS, PREFIXES, AND SUFFIXES

ANSWER:

Meaning: child, children
Examples: <u>ped</u>iatrician, <u>ped</u>agogue

---

26 GREEK ROOTS, PREFIXES, AND SUFFIXES

QUESTION: What is the meaning? Provide examples.

philo-, phil-

---

26 GREEK ROOTS, PREFIXES, AND SUFFIXES

ANSWER: Meaning: having a strong affinity or love for
Examples: <u>phil</u>anthropy, <u>phil</u>harmonic, <u>philo</u>sophy

---

27 GREEK ROOTS, PREFIXES, AND SUFFIXES

QUESTION: What is the meaning? Provide examples.

-phile

---

27 GREEK ROOTS, PREFIXES, AND SUFFIXES

ANSWER:

Meaning: one that loves or has a strong affinity for; loving
Examples: audio<u>phile</u>, Franco<u>phile</u>

---

28 GREEK ROOTS, PREFIXES, AND SUFFIXES

QUESTION: What is the meaning? Provide examples.

-phobe, -phobia

---

28 GREEK ROOTS, PREFIXES, AND SUFFIXES

ANSWER: Meaning: one who fears a specified thing; an intense fear of a specified thing
Examples: claustro<u>phobia</u>, arachno<u>phobe</u>, xeno<u>phobia</u>

GREEK ROOTS, PREFIXES, AND SUFFIXES

Inside-Outside Circle

Instructions. Cut out the Greek Roots, Prefixes, and Suffixes cards and use them to quiz a partner in Inside-Outside Circle.

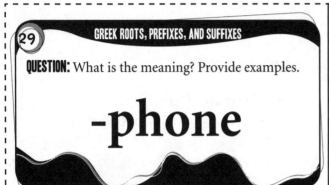

29 GREEK ROOTS, PREFIXES, AND SUFFIXES

QUESTION: What is the meaning? Provide examples.

-phone

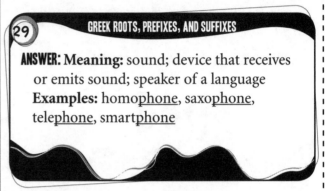

29 GREEK ROOTS, PREFIXES, AND SUFFIXES

ANSWER: Meaning: sound; device that receives or emits sound; speaker of a language
Examples: homo<u>phone</u>, saxo<u>phone</u>, tele<u>phone</u>, smart<u>phone</u>

30 GREEK ROOTS, PREFIXES, AND SUFFIXES

QUESTION: What is the meaning? Provide examples.

pan-

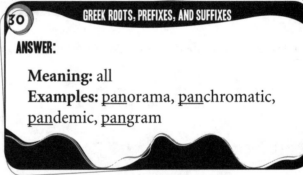

30 GREEK ROOTS, PREFIXES, AND SUFFIXES

ANSWER:

Meaning: all
Examples: <u>pan</u>orama, <u>pan</u>chromatic, <u>pan</u>demic, <u>pan</u>gram

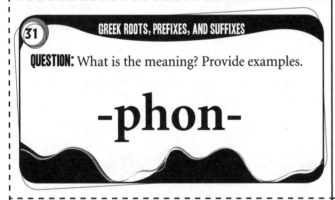

31 GREEK ROOTS, PREFIXES, AND SUFFIXES

QUESTION: What is the meaning? Provide examples.

-phon-

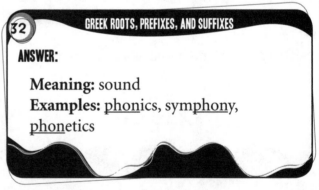

32 GREEK ROOTS, PREFIXES, AND SUFFIXES

ANSWER:

Meaning: sound
Examples: <u>phon</u>ics, sym<u>phon</u>y, <u>phon</u>etics

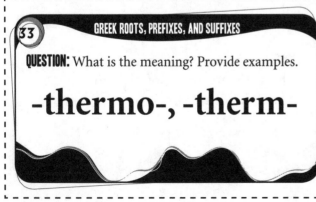

33 GREEK ROOTS, PREFIXES, AND SUFFIXES

QUESTION: What is the meaning? Provide examples.

-thermo-, -therm-

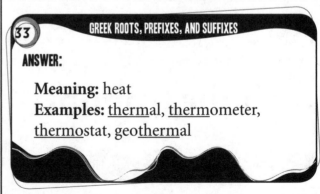

33 GREEK ROOTS, PREFIXES, AND SUFFIXES

ANSWER:

Meaning: heat
Examples: <u>therm</u>al, <u>therm</u>ometer, <u>therm</u>ostat, geo<u>thermal</u>

ANIMAL CELL CARDS
Inside-Outside Circle

Instructions. Display the Animal Cell Illustration. Use these cards to quiz a partner in Inside-Outside Circle.

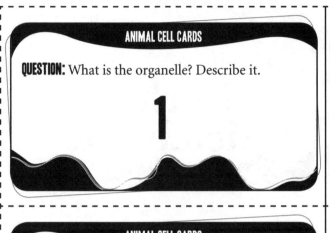

ANIMAL CELL CARDS

QUESTION: What is the organelle? Describe it.

1

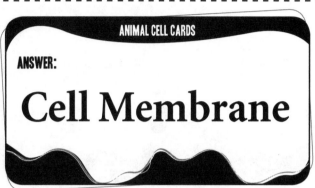

ANIMAL CELL CARDS

ANSWER:

Cell Membrane

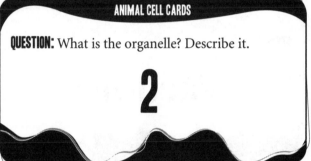

ANIMAL CELL CARDS

QUESTION: What is the organelle? Describe it.

2

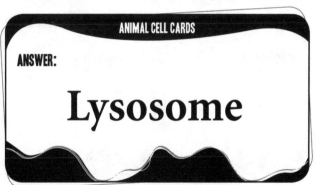

ANIMAL CELL CARDS

ANSWER:

Lysosome

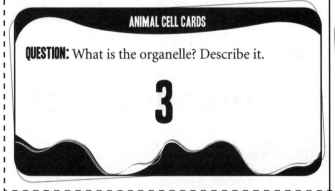

ANIMAL CELL CARDS

QUESTION: What is the organelle? Describe it.

3

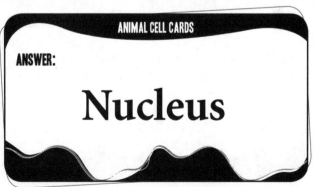

ANIMAL CELL CARDS

ANSWER:

Nucleus

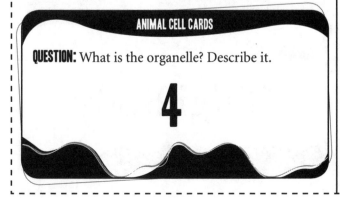

ANIMAL CELL CARDS

QUESTION: What is the organelle? Describe it.

4

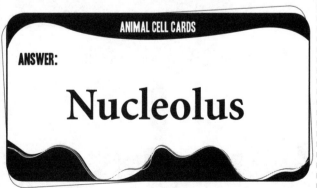

ANIMAL CELL CARDS

ANSWER:

Nucleolus

Instructions. Display the Animal Cell Illustration. Use these cards to quiz a partner in Inside-Outside Circle.

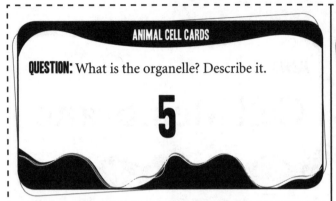

ANIMAL CELL CARDS

QUESTION: What is the organelle? Describe it.

5

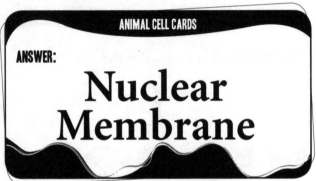

ANIMAL CELL CARDS

ANSWER:

Nuclear Membrane

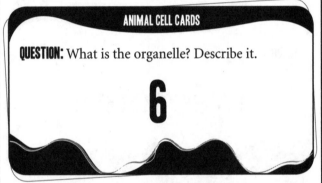

ANIMAL CELL CARDS

QUESTION: What is the organelle? Describe it.

6

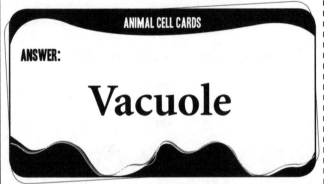

ANIMAL CELL CARDS

ANSWER:

Vacuole

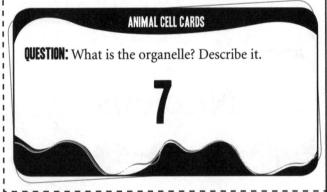

ANIMAL CELL CARDS

QUESTION: What is the organelle? Describe it.

7

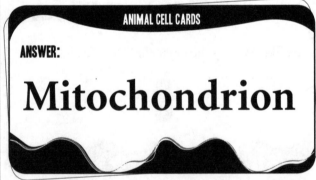

ANIMAL CELL CARDS

ANSWER:

Mitochondrion

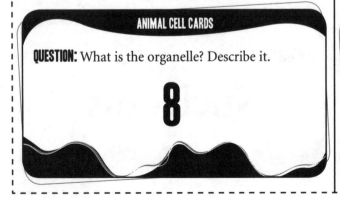

ANIMAL CELL CARDS

QUESTION: What is the organelle? Describe it.

8

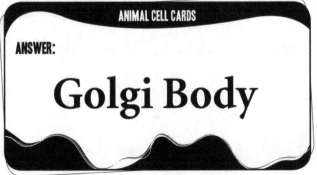

ANIMAL CELL CARDS

ANSWER:

Golgi Body

ANIMAL CELL CARDS

Inside-Outside Circle

Instructions. Display the Animal Cell Illustration. Use these cards to quiz a partner in Inside-Outside Circle.

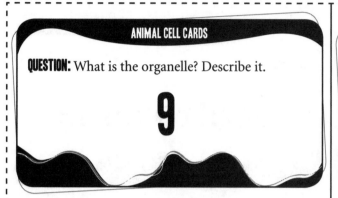

ANIMAL CELL CARDS

QUESTION: What is the organelle? Describe it.

9

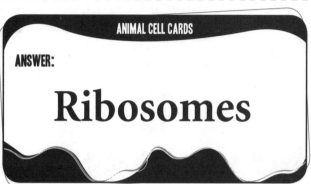

ANIMAL CELL CARDS

ANSWER:

Ribosomes

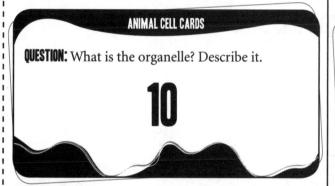

ANIMAL CELL CARDS

QUESTION: What is the organelle? Describe it.

10

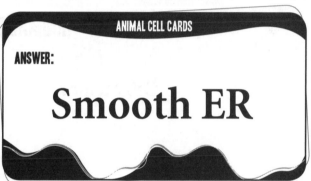

ANIMAL CELL CARDS

ANSWER:

Smooth ER

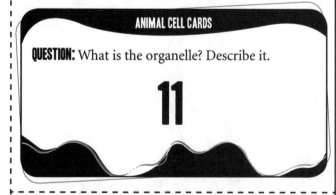

ANIMAL CELL CARDS

QUESTION: What is the organelle? Describe it.

11

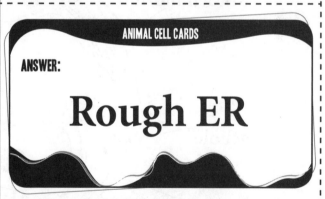

ANIMAL CELL CARDS

ANSWER:

Rough ER

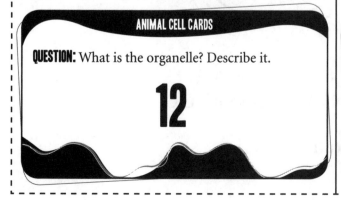

ANIMAL CELL CARDS

QUESTION: What is the organelle? Describe it.

12

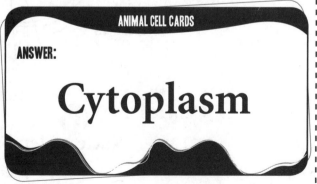

ANIMAL CELL CARDS

ANSWER:

Cytoplasm

 ANIMAL CELL CARDS

Inside-Outside Circle

Instructions. Display the Animal Cell Illustration. Use these cards to quiz a partner in Inside-Outside Circle.

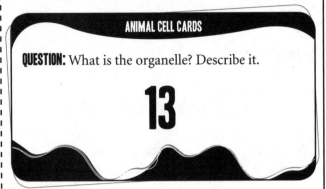

ANIMAL CELL CARDS

QUESTION: What is the organelle? Describe it.

13

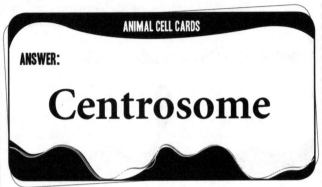

ANIMAL CELL CARDS

ANSWER:

Centrosome

ANIMAL CELL ANSWERS

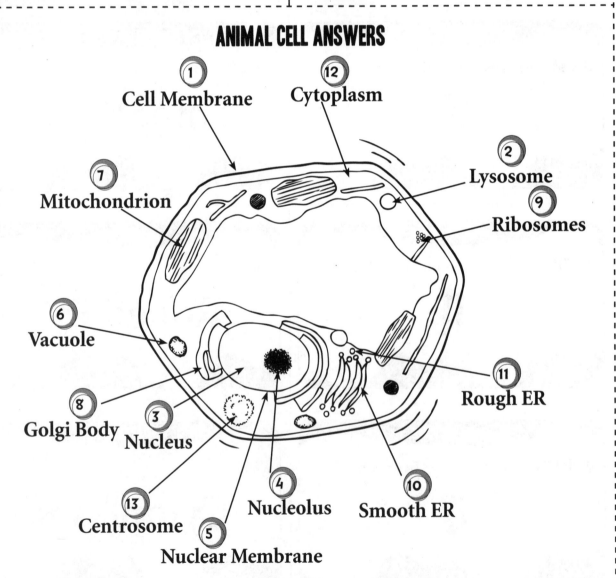

1. Cell Membrane
12. Cytoplasm
2. Lysosome
9. Ribosomes
7. Mitochondrion
11. Rough ER
6. Vacuole
8. Golgi Body
3. Nucleus
13. Centrosome
5. Nuclear Membrane
4. Nucleolus
10. Smooth ER

ANIMAL CELL ILLUSTRATION

Inside-Outside Circle

Teacher Instructions. Display this Animal Cell Illustration for the class as they play Inside-Outside Circle using the Animal Cell Cards.

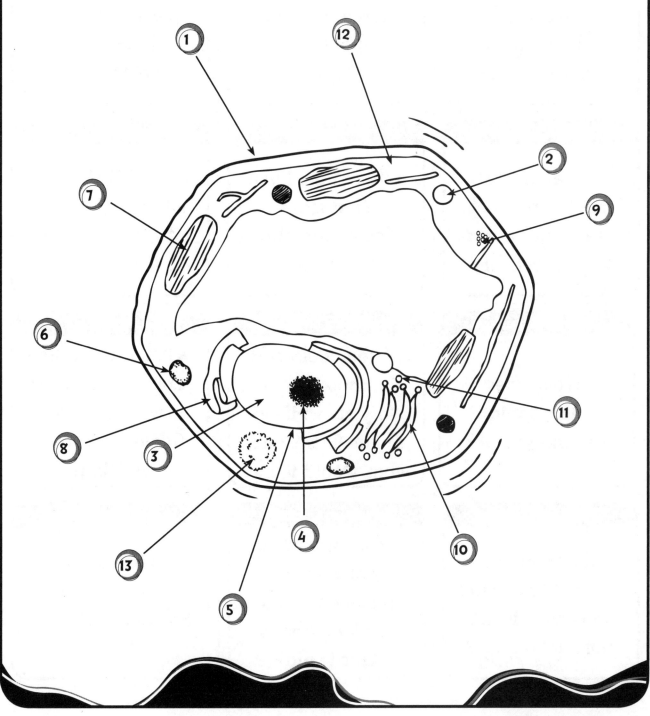

PREWRITING QUESTION CARDS
Inside-Outside Circle

Instructions. Make enough copies of this blackline so that each student has one card. Cut out the question cards and give each student one card. Students use cards to ask partners prewriting questions during Inside-Outside Circle.

Prewriting Questions What topic are you planning to write about?	**Prewriting Questions** What do you already know about this topic?	**Prewriting Questions** What questions do you still have about this topic?
Prewriting Questions What is the most important idea to get across to your readers?	**Prewriting Questions** Where could you find more information about this topic?	**Prewriting Questions** What will readers find interesting about this topic?
Prewriting Questions What does this topic remind you of?	**Prewriting Questions** If you could add a photograph to your writing about this topic, what would it be?	**Prewriting Questions** What information about this topic will you not include in your writing?
Prewriting Questions How can you present the topic so that it is not boring to read?	**Prewriting Questions** What words do you want to include in your writing about this topic?	**Prewriting Questions** What would be a good title for your writing? Why?

SOURCE: Skidmore, S. & Graber, J. *Balanced Literacy Grade 5*. San Clemente, CA: Kagan Publishing.

Structure #11

INSTANT STAR

Structure #11
INSTANT STAR

Students are randomly selected to be the "Instant Star" of their team. Stars stand to applause and share with their teammates.

STEPS   Getting Ready
The teacher prepares question(s).

Step 1 Teacher Asks Question

The teacher asks the class a question. The question can be a simple review question such as, "*Where did the first Gulf War take place?*" Or the question can be a thinking question such as, "*Do you think the first Gulf War was justified? Why or why not?*"

Step 2 Think Time

The teacher calls for Think Time and gives students 3–5 seconds of silent time to formulate their answers. "*Everyone think of your best response. No talking.*"

Step 3 Teacher Selects "Stars"

The teacher randomly selects one student on each team to be the Instant Star. "*Student #3's, you're the Instant Star. Teammates applaud for Student #3 as they stand.*"

59 Kagan Structures
Kagan Publishing • 1 (800) 933-2667 • KaganOnline.com

TIPS

- **Student Selector.** Use a student selector to randomly select the Instant Star.

- **Create Suspense.** Say something like, "*Let's see who will be the next Instant Star.*"

- **Elicit Applause.** Say something like, "*I will spin the spinner. We will give wild applause for whoever's number comes up. Why? Because they are the Instant Stars!*"

- **Manage Timing.** Tell Instant Stars to sit down when they are done sharing. Don't wait until the last Star is seated to continue with the lesson. When about two-thirds or three-fourths of the Stars are seated, say "*Most Stars are finished, everyone take a seat, and class let's hear it for the Instant Stars!*"

Step 4 — Stars Share with Teammates

Stars stand and share their thoughts or answers with teammates. They sit when done, so the teacher can tell when everyone is ready to proceed. "*Stars, please share your response with your team. Sit when you're done sharing.*"

Step 5 — Praise or Coach

For high-consensus (right or wrong) questions, teammates praise the Star if the answer is correct; if incorrect, teammates coach the Star. For low-consensus questions (thinking questions), teammates praise or comment on the thinking that went into the answer. "*I agree that Saddam had no right to invade Kuwait, and that the first Gulf War was justified to liberate Kuwait. You are a logical thinker!*"

Instant Star

Teacher Instructions. Spin this spinner to randomly select a student on the team to be the Instant Star. "*The Instant Star is student number …*"

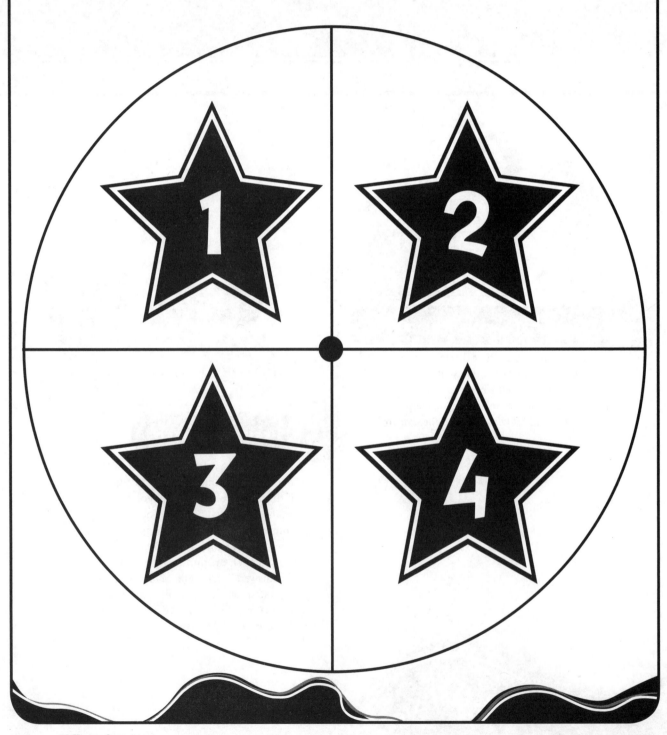

JOT THOUGHTS

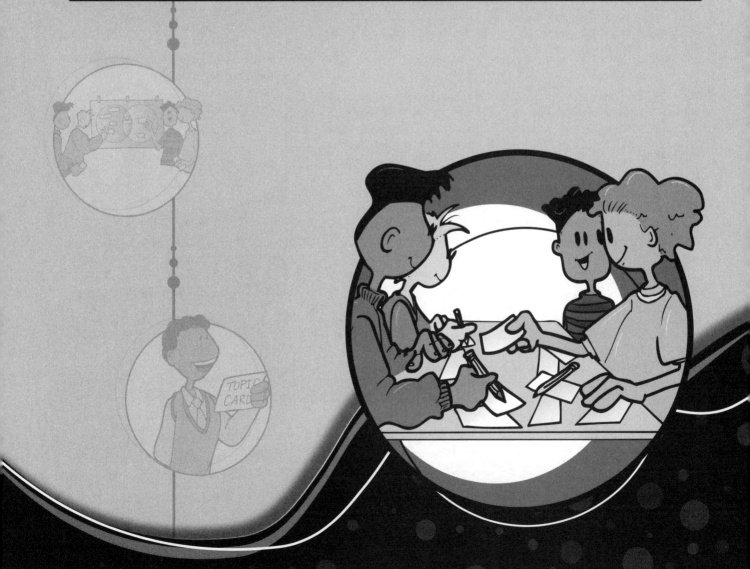

JOT THOUGHTS

Students brainstorm in teams, each teammate simultaneously writes ideas, with each idea on a separate slip of paper.

JOT THOUGHTS is a terrific way for teams to generate many ideas quickly. Teammates write an idea on a slip of paper, and announce it to the team. The team covers the table with ideas. The ideas can be solutions to a social problem, "*How can we end racism?*" The ideas can be solutions to a curriculum problem, "*What are the many ways to form the number 24?*" The ideas can be a list of examples, "*What might you find in a rain forest?*" The ideas can be representations of a type or category of items, "*List as many adjectives as you can.*" Often, the goal of brainstorming is to generate ideas from which to choose, "*What should be the topic of our team presentation?*" The best idea is not always the first idea that comes to mind. Sometimes the best idea is hidden in the depths of the mind, and brainstorming draws forth many ideas from students' minds onto paper, so students may select that one perfect solution.

When Jot Thoughts is used for brainstorming creative ideas, the basic rules of brainstorming apply. The ideas are deliberately as diverse as possible. Students need to think "out of the box." Funny, silly, and even wacky ideas are encouraged. They may not be the final solution, but they may help lead to it. Students need to suspend judgment on the ideas. Evaluation is the killer of creativity. During Jot Thoughts, neither criticism, nor praise of ideas is allowed. The goal is to simply get as many ideas as possible out of students' heads and onto slips. During brainstorming, students don't discuss or elaborate on ideas. There is a time for elaboration and evaluation, but that time is after the brainstorming.

Jot Thoughts has some distinct advantages over independent brainstorming. Students with different mindsets, backgrounds, and experiences generate a broader range of ideas. Plus, there is the power of synergy—the interaction of ideas is greater than the sum of independent ideas. Students announce each idea to teammates to unleash synergy. An idea by one teammate may trigger ideas for others. Spreading the ideas out on the table gives students instant access to all the ideas at any point, so they can piggyback on an idea or direction.

DIFFERENTIATED INSTRUCTION

- Students can draw a symbol of their idea rather than writing it.
- Students may be assigned a teammate to work with them as a buddy, to help them articulate, or record their ideas.

BENEFITS

Students...

…generate many possibilities quickly.

…participate in heterogeneous groups that have a broad base of backgrounds and experiences from which to draw.

…build on the ideas of teammates.

…develop creativity.

…learn to generate many possible ideas or solutions.

STEPS

Getting Ready: *The teacher prepares a brainstorming topic. Each student needs a pen and slips of paper.*

Step 1
Teacher Announces Topic

The teacher announces the brainstorming topic and sets a time limit. "*Brainstorm as many team names as you can. You have 3 minutes. First, announce your idea to the team. Second, write the team name on a slip of paper, and third, place the idea faceup on your team table. See if you can cover the table.*"

Step 2
Team Brainstorms

Teammates simultaneously generate as many ideas as they can in the allotted time. They write each idea on a separate slip of paper, announce the idea to teammates, and place the idea faceup on the team table. They attempt to "cover the table" rather than stacking the slips.

Step 3
Team Processes Ideas

When time's up, the team processes their brainstormed ideas. There are many ways to process ideas. How students process ideas depends on the goal of the brainstorming task. See What to Do with Ideas on page 68.

Jot Thoughts

VARIATION

• A–Z Brainstorming

Have students brainstorm an idea for each letter of the alphabet. Prior to brainstorming, students deal out A–Z Brainstorming Cards to teammates (see blackline). To brainstorm, they say it, write it, and place it. A–Z Brainstorming can be done also in teams using RoundTable or in pairs using RallyTable, with each student generating the next idea beginning with the next letter of the alphabet. For animals: anteater, bear, cougar, and so on.

WHAT TO DO WITH IDEAS

• **Organize Ideas.** Teams organize ideas using a graphic organizer or a chart.

• **Select Best Idea.** Teams pick their best idea among the ideas generated.

• **Prioritize Ideas.** Teams sequence ideas by priority.

• **Share Ideas.** Teams share ideas with other teams.

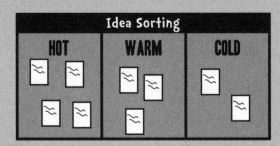

TIPS

• **Model.** Select a team, and model the Jot Thoughts process for the class.

• **Suspend Judgment.** Tell students not to censor their own ideas, criticize, or evaluate the ideas of others during brainstorming.

• **Suspend Discussion.** Students are not to discuss or elaborate on their ideas during the idea-generation phase.

• **Make It Fun.** Creativity thrives in a positive learning environment.

• **Color Code Contributions.** To encourage participation by all and to promote accountability for contribution by each student, have each student use a different colored pen or marker to record their ideas.

• **Time It.** Set a time limit to encourage speed, but don't make the time limit too short. Suggestion: 3 minutes.

• **Say It, Write It, Place It.** For each new idea, students say it first, so they are not writing redundant ideas. Then they write it on a slip of paper and place it on the team table. When introducing Jot Thoughts to students, use the expression, "*Say it, write it, place it*," so students know exactly what to do with their ideas.

• **Sorting Mat.** After Jot Thoughts, have students sort their ideas on an Idea Sorting Mat. See blacklines.

• **Brainstorming Tips.** Display for the class the brainstorming tips sheet provided on page 70. Reinforce the tips for effective brainstorming.

IDEAS Across the Curriculum

Mathematics

Students brainstorm…

- Word problems for a given equation
- Ways to build 20
- Applications of an algorithm
- Things that are square
- Symmetrical objects

Language Arts

Students brainstorm…

- Characters in a book/play
- Rhyming words
- Possible story endings
- Nouns
- Adjectives describing a character
- Possible topic sentences for a paragraph
- Words that start with *s*
- Words that have the "ch" sound
- Proper nouns
- Story character characteristics
- Events in the story

Social Studies

Students brainstorm…

- Events in the chapter/unit
- Historical figures in the era
- Landforms
- States
- Countries
- Facts about an event
- Community helpers
- Facts about a state
- Examples of change
- Differences between…
- How to solve a social issue
- Campaign ideas

Science

Students brainstorm…

- Mammals
- Possible outcomes of an experiment
- Hypotheses
- Vertebrates
- Constellations
- Bones/body parts
- Insects
- Examples of a law or principle…
- Similarities between…
- Objects with a simple machine

Music

Students brainstorm…

- Bands that meet a criterion
- String instruments
- Musical professions
- CDs students own
- Songs of a certain style
- Well-known musicians

Classbuilding and Teambuilding

Students brainstorm…

- Cartoons
- Type of cars
- Fun free time activities
- Water sports
- Qualities of a good friend/teammate
- Vacation spots
- Praising words
- Rainy day activities
- Favorite movies

Jot Thoughts

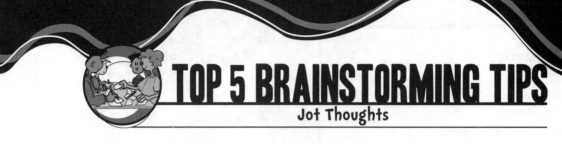

TOP 5 BRAINSTORMING TIPS
Jot Thoughts

Teacher Instructions. Use this sheet to teach students the Top 5 Brainstorming Tips.

❶ The More, the Merrier

Generate a lot of ideas. The more ideas you come up with, the more you'll have to choose from.

❷ Piggyback

Build on the ideas of others. Combine ideas. Create similar ideas. Use associations.

❸ Don't Judge

Don't discuss or criticize any ideas. Don't judge your own ideas. Put them out there. Evaluation can come later.

❹ Speed It Up

Write the first idea and every idea that comes to mind.

❺ Get Wacky

Include creative, unusual, and silly ideas.

59 Kagan Structures
Kagan Publishing • 1 (800) 933-2667 • KaganOnline.com

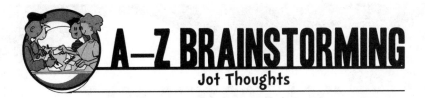

A–Z BRAINSTORMING
Jot Thoughts

Instructions. Cut out one set of letter cards for each student to use for A–Z Brainstorming.

A	B	C	D
E	F	G	H
I	J	K	L
M	N	O	P
Q	R	S	T
U	V	W	X
Y	Z		

Possible Topics:

- Animals
- Food
- Movies
- Countries
- Careers
- Teams
- Books
- Characters
- Historical events

IDEA SORTING MAT

Jot Thoughts

Instructions. Use this Idea Sorting Mat to sort the ideas your team brainstormed.

HOT (GREAT)	WARM (GOOD)	COLD (SO-SO)

59 Kagan Structures
Kagan Publishing • 1 (800) 933-2667 • KaganOnline.com

YES-NO-MAYBE SORTING
Jot Thoughts

Instructions. Use this mat to sort the ideas your team brainstormed into Yes, No, and Maybe categories.

YES

NO

MAYBE

TOPIC MAT

Jot Thoughts

Instructions. Write your topic in the center. Write the subtopic in each section. As a team, brainstorm ideas and write them in the subtopic section in which they belong.

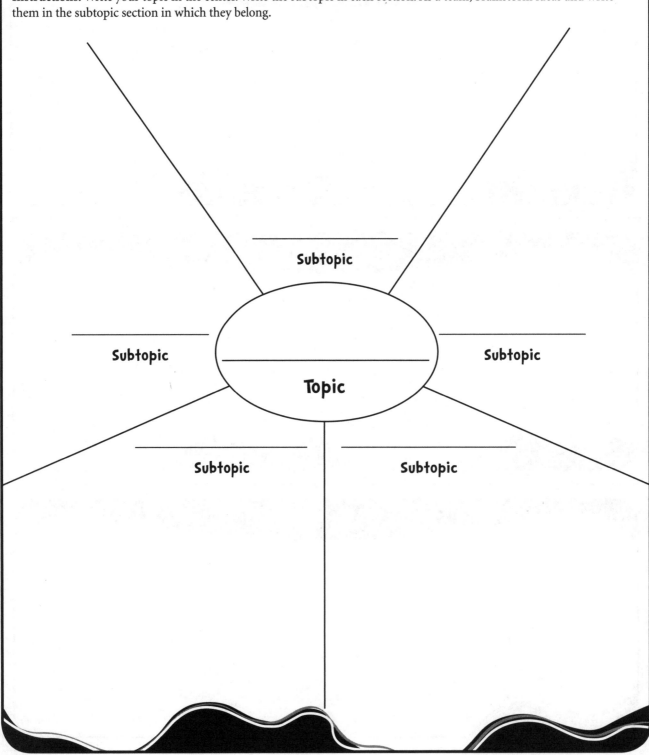

Subtopic

Subtopic

Subtopic

Topic

Subtopic

Subtopic

Structure #13

KINESTHETIC SYMBOLS

Structure #13
KINESTHETIC SYMBOLS

Students create and practice hand or body symbols associated with the content.

STEPS

Getting Ready
The teacher selects the words or topics for the Kinesthetic Symbols.

Step 1 Create Symbols

The teacher prepares the symbols for the class, or students work in teams to create symbols to represent the content. The symbols are hands or whole-body motions. For example, to learn geometry terms, students use their hands or arms to represent terms such as: parallel, perpendicular, acute angle, right angle, obtuse angle, and straight angle.

Step 2 Students Practice Symbols

Students practice using the symbols. When the teacher prepares the symbols, the teacher asks questions of the class, and the class responds by sharing the symbol. Or, when students develop their own symbols, teams can share their symbols with the class or with other teams. Students can take turns leading the team in a review of the symbols. For example, Student #1 takes the team's list of geometry terms and quizzes teammates on the symbols. *"What is the symbol for parallel? What is the symbol for a right angle?"*

Using Symbols and Signals

In the Classroom
- Symbolize curriculum
- Communicate basic needs
- Manage the class
- Finger numbers
- Response Modes

Beyond the Classroom
- Machinery operation
- Sports plays
- Sports officials/referees
- Animal/obedience training
- Scuba diving
- Road safety
- Military
- Police/SWAT

Content Possibilities

- Punctuation
- Steps of procedure
- Steps of algorithm
- Steps: bill becomes law
- Parts of a letter
- Water cycle
- Parts of a bill
- Bill of Rights

MANAGEMENT SIGNALS
Kinesthetic Symbols

Instructions. Use these illustrations to share management signals with your class.

Quiet Signal

Over My Head

Slow Down

Can't Hear

Can't See

Question or Share

Repeat

Good Work

Still Thinking

Instructions. Use these hand symbols to represent geometry terms.

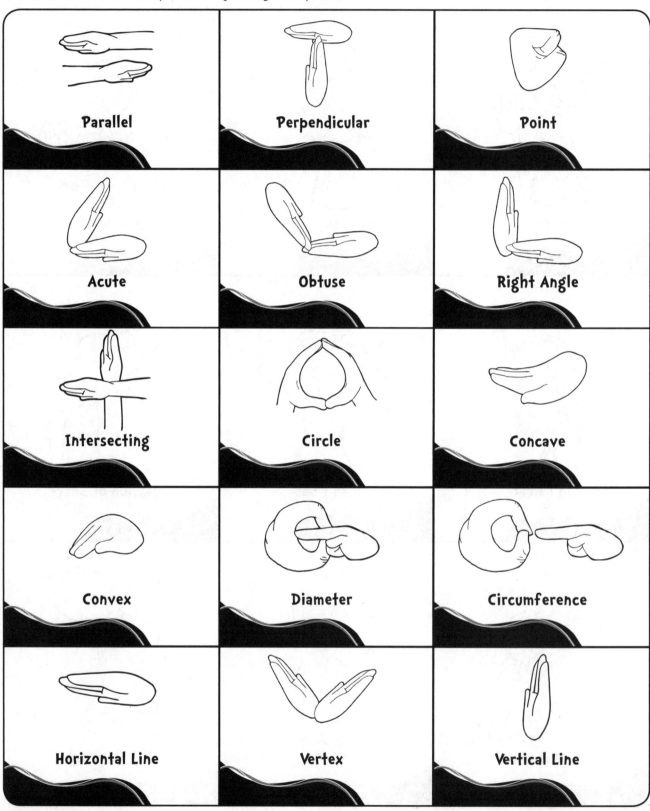

Parallel	Perpendicular	Point
Acute	Obtuse	Right Angle
Intersecting	Circle	Concave
Convex	Diameter	Circumference
Horizontal Line	Vertex	Vertical Line

LISTEN RIGHT!

Structure #14
LISTEN RIGHT!

During a lecture, the teacher stops. Students write
the main points, compare with a partner, and celebrate.

STUDENTS LEARN and remember more when lectures are punctuated with brief processing breaks. Listen Right! does just that—it periodically interrupts a lecture for students to process their new learning. Further, the types of processing involved takes maximum advantage of many principles of learning and memory. To use Listen Right! the instructor stops lecturing after a period (3–5 minutes for elementary, 5–15 minutes for secondary). Students pick up their pens and write the key points of the lecture so far. Then, students form pairs or small groups. They take turns sharing what they learned, using RallyRobin, RoundRobin, Instant Star, or Timed Pair Share. Next, the instructor quickly reviews the key points. Students celebrate with their partners if they covered all the key points or add them if they missed any. Then the teacher resumes the lecture. The teacher stops after a few minutes and students process the new material.

There are some powerful learning principles at work here. First is Understanding. Students have the opportunity to process new learning and develop an understanding of its meaning. Without processing, students may not really grasp what is being taught. Worse than fuzzy or incomplete understanding is misunderstanding. The brain will cling just as tenaciously to wrong ideas as it will to right ones. So it is important for students to learn it correctly the first time, otherwise learning requires unlearning and relearning—a much more difficult process. By review of the material in many ways, students gain a concise understanding of the content, and come away with a correct understanding the first time. The next principle is Recitation. Recitation is the process of "repeating" the learning and is one of the strongest techniques for long-term content retention. Repeating can occur by thinking about, writing, or verbalizing the content. Verbalizing is probably the strongest since it incorporates both the vocal and auditory senses. Students do all three in Listen Right! Overlearning is another principle Listen Right! incorporates. Overlearning is the principle that after we understand or master a concept, we may engrave the mental trace deeper and deeper in our brains by processing it again. The more we learn the material, the better our chances of establishing a base for long-term retention. Through the many forms of recitation, plus the teacher's review, students are on their way to overlearning the content.

The analogy that the brain is like a cup of water serves as a good visual image. When the cup is full, pouring in more water is fruitless. It spills over the cup. The brain is temporarily full and not ready for new learning. We empty the cup by pouring out the water. And we prepare the brain for new learning by allowing it to process new learning, moving it from working to longer-term memory. After brief processing breaks, students are more likely to recall past learning and are more receptive to new learning.

DIFFERENTIATED INSTRUCTION

- Students can draw rather than write their responses.
- Students may be assigned a buddy to help them articulate and/ or record their responses.

BENEFITS

Students...

...retain more of what they learn.

...find lectures more engaging and less boring.

...process learning in many ways.

...are accountable for listening carefully to the lecture.

...receive feedback on note taking while teachers are not lecturing.

STEPS

Getting Ready
The teacher prepares discussion topics.

Step 1 — Teacher Lectures

The teacher lectures while students listen carefully without taking notes.

Step 2 — Students Write Key Points

After a short period of lecture, the teacher stops. Students write the key points of the lecture.

Step 3 — Partners Share Key Points

The teacher asks students to pair up and share with a partner, checking for accuracy and making corrections on their own papers. To share, they may use Timed Pair Share to take equal timed turns to share, or they use RallyRobin or Pair Share where students alternate sharing a key point.

Step 4 — Teacher Reviews Key Points

The teacher reviews the key points just shared. Students record any additional points that they missed.

Step 5 — Partners Celebrate

Partners celebrate with a praiser or celebration.

Step 6 — Continue Process

The teacher resumes lecturing for a short period, then stops again for students to take notes and process the new content. Usually only part of the lecture is punctuated with Listen Right!

Listen Right!

STRUCTURE POWER

Listen Right! creates intense focus: When it's time to listen, students listen intently. Their attention is not divided by trying to take notes at the same time. And when it's time to take notes, they focus on writing notes without having to also listen for new, competing information. Listen Right! takes more time than the traditional take-notes-while-the-teacher-lectures format, however the occasional use of Listen Right! fosters skills not developed in the traditional format. Instead of writing everything the teacher says, students are forced to hold chunks of content in short-term memory. They must evaluate, asking themselves which are the key points. There are a number of additional benefits of Listen Right! In the traditional classroom, there is no accountability or feedback for the quality of note taking. Some students take few or even no notes. That cannot happen in Listen Right! because the structure holds students accountable for writing and provides immediate feedback. With Listen Right! students benefit from peer modeling, tutoring, coaching, and encouragement—all absent with traditional lecture/note taking formats. Having been held accountable for and having received feedback on their note taking, students take better notes following Listen Right! even in the traditional format. Another benefit of Listen Right! is that it activates two powerful memory principles: Primacy and Recency. In the traditional lecture, there is one beginning and one end; with Listen Right! there are many beginnings and many endings; the chunked lecture multiplies powerful primacy and recency effects to enhance memory. Yet another reason Listen Right! is powerful: Frequent pauses allow the teacher to walk around observing and listening in as students interact with the content. This provides authentic assessment of student learning and allows the teacher to adjust if necessary. Finally, not to be underestimated: Lectures are improved! Why? When we frequently pause during our lectures, we better compose what we are going to say next.

TIPS

• **Prime Students.** Tell students in advance to listen carefully to the lecture because they will have to remember and share what they hear.

• **Plan Breaks.** While planning the lecture, look for good break points that will break the lecture into like concepts in acceptable time chunks.

• **Lecture Duration.** In a traditional lecture, a good rule of thumb is that the lecture should be punctuated by processing time about every 10 minutes, somewhat longer for easy content and older students, and shorter for difficult content and younger students. Listen Right! is different. Because the students are not taking notes while the lecture is going, the teacher must stop more frequently—Usually about every 3 to 5 minutes. For this reason, Listen Right! is used only as part of a long lecture, not the whole lecture. It is a strong addition to a traditional lecture used to emphasize and ensure mastery and memory of important points.

• **Cloze Form.** The teacher may provide students with a form with blanks to fill in missing key words from the lecture.

• **Outline.** The teacher may provide students with an outline of the lecture that students complete when the teacher pauses.

Periodically stop lecturing to allow time for student processing.

VARIATIONS

- **Draw Right!** The lecture is punctuated with intermissions for students to draw the key points.

- **Map Right!** The lecture is punctuated with intermissions for students to mind map the central concept.

- **Cover Those Notes!** Students are allowed to take notes during the lectures, but must cover them when they are to share key points in Step 2.

FLOWCHART OF LISTEN RIGHT!

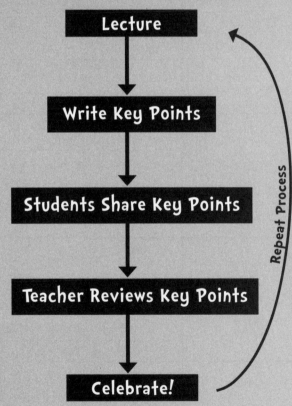

Lecture

↓

Write Key Points

↓

Students Share Key Points

↓

Teacher Reviews Key Points

↓

Celebrate!

Repeat Process

Listen Right!

NOTE TAKING PAGE
Listen Right!

TOPIC_____ DATE_____

KEY IDEAS	NOTES

59 Kagan Structures
Kagan Publishing • 1 (800) 933-2667 • KaganOnline.com

KEY IDEAS
Listen Right!

Topic _____   Date _____

Part #1

Part #2

Part #3

Part #4

KEY POINTS
Listen Right!

TOPIC_____ DATE_____

PROCESSING #1	PROCESSING #2
My Key Points	**My Key Points**
_____ _____ _____ _____ _____	_____ _____ _____ _____ _____
Partner's Key Points	**Partner's Key Points**
_____ _____ _____ _____ _____	_____ _____ _____ _____ _____
Teacher's Key Points	**Teacher's Key Points**
_____ _____ _____ _____ _____	_____ _____ _____ _____ _____

NUMBERED HEADS TOGETHER

Structure #15
NUMBERED HEADS TOGETHER

Teammates put their "heads together" to discuss the question and make sure everyone knows the answer. One teammate's number is randomly called, and that teammate shares the team's answer.

IN TEAMS, students number off so each student has a number: one, two, three, four (thus the name "Numbered"). The teacher asks a question. The question can be a high-consensus, right-or-wrong question such as: "*What is the distance to the moon?*" Or it can be a problem to be worked out by the team: "*Convert 650 feet per second into miles per hour.*" The question can also be a low-consensus discussion question like: "*Do you think there is extraterrestrial life?*" For individual accountability, students independently write their own answers. Students stand up and huddle together (thus the name "Heads Together") to show what they have written, and/or discuss the question. The teacher then calls on a number. The student with the number called is responsible for giving the team's answer or summarizing what the team discussed.

Numbered Heads Together is a powerful antidote to the traditional review session. All students become active during the question and answer. Each student is accountable for writing an answer to each question, and each student knows he or she may be called upon to share the team's answer or summarize the team's discussion.

DIFFERENTIATED INSTRUCTION

- Students can draw their answers.
- The teacher can call on students to repeat or explain the answers given by others.
- The teacher can call on students to agree with or disagree with an answer using a thumbs up or sideways signal, and then call on students to explain why. Thus, students do not have to generate an answer. Instead, having just heard it, they simply explain why they agree or disagree.
- If a teacher numbers the students by their ability, the teacher can ask developmentally differentiated questions, asking for the appropriate ability group number to respond.

BENEFITS

Students...

...are each responsible for learning and sharing.

...receive frequent and immediate feedback.

...are on the same side as teammates and hope for each other's success.

...stay on their toes because they write and share their answers, and each knows they may be called on.

59 Kagan Structures
Kagan Publishing • 1 (800) 933-2667 • KaganOnline.com

Getting Ready: *The teacher prepares questions or problems to ask teams. Students have response boards or individual think slips and writing utensils.*

STEPS

Step 1 Students Number Off

Students number off in their teams from 1–4.

Step 2 Teacher Asks a Question and Provides Think Time

The teacher asks a question or poses a problem and provides Think Time. The question can be a question with a right or wrong answer such as "*What is the sequence of colors in a visible color spectrum?*" Or the question can be an open-ended discussion question like "*What conditions make the formation of a rainbow more likely and why? Everyone think about your answer.*"

continued

Step 3 Individuals Write

Students privately write their answers, no talking.

Numbered Heads Together

STEPS (Continued)

Step 4 — Heads Together

Students lift up from their chairs to put their heads together, show answers, and discuss and teach. Students reach a consensus on the team's answer and make sure they all know the team's answer because one of them will be selected to represent the team.

Step 5 — Students Sit

Students sit down when everyone knows the answer or has something to share. Students erase their boards or hide their answers (so they must individually re-solve or recall the answer if selected).

4!

Step 6 — Teacher Calls a Number

The teacher randomly calls a student number from 1–4. All selected students stand. The teacher asks standing students the question (or a similar question).

59 Kagan Structures
Kagan Publishing • 1 (800) 933-2667 • KaganOnline.com

Step 7 Selected Students Solve the Problem

The standing students independently solve the problem and write the answer(s) on their boards. The teacher calls "*Show Me,*" then the selected student on each team holds up his or her response board.

Step 8 Class Praises Respondents

Classmates cheer the students who responded.

Numbered Heads Together

STRUCTURE POWER

Numbered Heads Together is classic cooperative learning. It has positive interdependence: One student knowing the answer helps the others, and all students must do their part for the team to be successful. There is individual accountability: Students must write their answers on their own, and a quarter of the time they are called upon to answer in front of the class. There is virtually equal participation: All write; students are called upon about equally. And finally, there is simultaneous interaction: In contrast to the traditional classroom in which only one student responds to the question and the others are free to tune out, in Numbered Heads Together, every student writes his or her answer—100 percent of the students respond to the question, not just one in the class! It is no wonder that when teachers abandon the traditional question-answer format, and switch to Numbered Heads Together, their classrooms become a beehive of active engagement and achievement accelerates.

TIPS

• **Random Numbers.** Make Numbered Heads Together more game-like by randomly calling a student number by spinning a spinner, rolling a die, pulling numbers from a hat, throwing a dart at a dartboard (with four sections), or using an electronic student selector.

• **Individuals Write.** Make sure students think and write their own answers and share them with the group to increase participation and accountability. Chalkboards or individual AnswerBoards work great for students to write and share their answers.

• **Clean Slate.** Have students clean their slates or boards or hide their notes after the team has shared and before the number is called.

• **Teams Sit.** Having teams sit once they are done is a great visual cue. If most teams are still standing, then they need more time to work on the problem or it's time to reteach.

• **Different Numbered Teams.** If you have some teams of three and/or five, you'll have to change the rules a little. In teams of three, Students #3's answer when number four is selected. In teams of five, Students #4 and #5 take turns answering when #4 is called.

• **Scoring.** Teams may earn points for correct answers and the points may be summed toward a class goal.

Mathematics

- What is your definition of a ___?
- Make change from money given
- Calender questions
- Where is my mistake?
- Use manipulatives to represent the number or problem
- Read graphs
- Build a math problem with manipulatives
- Draw out a solution
- Measure objects
- Solve word problems
- Write a word problem to represent an equation
- Plot numbers on graph or number line
- Draw conclusions from the data or graphs shown

Language Arts

- Spelling words
- Main idea of a paragraph
- Good ending for the story
- Adjectives to describe…
- Correct grammar mistakes
- Skim page—What do you think it's about?
- Describe events in a story or book
- Identify part of speech
- Simile or metaphor
- Appropriate end mark
- Generate a good topic sentence for the paragraph
- Define a vocabulary word

Social Studies

- Community helpers
- How did Native Americans use these tools?
- Vocabulary words
- Land formations questions
- Difference past/now
- Answer review questions for a chapter
- Identify a state based on geographical descriptions
- Describe a historical event
- Identify the branch of government
- Describe characteristics of a culture
- Identify the cause or effect

Science

- Animals
- Parts of plants
- Review steps of experiment
- Rain forest
- Steps of cell division
- Seasons
- Principles or laws
- Answer questions about the experiment
- Identify an element based on characteristics
- Describe what would happen if…
- Define a term, law, or principle
- Draw or define cell part
- Identify the state of matter

Music

- What instruments do you hear in this piece?

Art

- What is the artist trying to convey?

Physical Education

- Review rules of the game

VARIATIONS

Response Modes. Step 7 calls for students to share their team's answer simultaneously. A variety of possible response modes can be used, depending on the type of question, including the following:

- **Thumbs Up, Thumbs Down.** For yes or no, or agree or disagree answers, all students selected answer simultaneously with a thumb up for yes or agree, or a thumb down for no or disagree.

- **Slates and Response Boards.** It is ideal for each student to have a response board. That way, students can independently write their answers on their boards, and then use their boards to share with the class when selected. When a number is called to select one student from each team, that student writes the answer on the team slate or board, and shares it with the class.

$$4+x=12$$
$$x=8$$

- **Response Cards.** All selected students hold up a response card (such as Yes or No).

- **Finger Responses.** Selected students hold up the number of fingers to indicate their answers.

- **Kinesthetic Symbols.** Students respond with predetermined Kinesthetic Symbols to show the answer.

- **Teams Post.** All selected students write the team answer on a designated area of the class whiteboard.

- **Choral Response.** All selected students say the answer in unison.

- **Discussion Questions.** If it is a discussion question, call on a few different teams to get a range of ideas discussed.

- **Shared Responses.** If the question has multiple parts, choose a different team or a different number to answer each part.

- **Adding On.** If a response is incomplete, select another team to add on. "*Team 6, what can you add to the answer?*"

- **Agree or Disagree.** One of the many standing students is selected to share his or her team's answer. If the other standing students agree, they sit down. If they disagree, they remain standing and the teacher can call on one to share a different answer. Alternatively, teams use Agree and Disagree response boards or cards. The teacher can call on a team displaying Disagree.

RELATED STRUCTURES

#16 Paired Heads Together

In each team, students have face partners and shoulder partners. Each pairing consists of a Partner A and Partner B. The teacher asks a question, provides Think Time, and students independently write their answers. They first pair up with their shoulder partners to share answers and coach if necessary. The teacher randomly calls, "A" or "B." Then, the selected partners share their answers with their face partners.

 Teacher Assigns Pairs

The teacher distinguishes shoulder partners from face partners. Shoulder partners are students sitting next to each other on the team. Face partners are students sitting across from each other on the team.

 Teacher Asks Question

The teacher presents a problem or question and provides Think Time.

 Students Write

Students write their answers individually, without help.

 Share and Discuss

Students share and discuss their answers with their shoulder partners, coaching if necessary.

 Students Signal

Students signal when ready. Probably the best signal is to have students stand when they share and sit when done. This provides a great visual signal, and the standing and sitting keeps their brains awake.

 Students Share

The teacher says, "*Turn to your face partner. As, share your best answer. Bs, just listen.*" Students share as individuals, face partner to face partner, not pair to pair.

 Teacher Gives Answer

The teacher announces answer, saying, "*If your partner said X, then give your partner a high five (hug, hand shake...).*"

 Repeat

The teacher does additional rounds, mixing up each time which face partner answers.

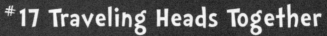

#17 Traveling Heads Together

Traveling Heads Together is Numbered Heads Together with a traveling component. It starts the same as Numbered Heads Together. The teacher presents a problem. Students independently think about their answer, then privately write their answers. Then, everyone on the team stands and puts their heads together to reach consensus on the answer. They sit when everyone agrees on the team's answer. The teacher randomly calls a number 1–4 and all students with that number stand. Now here's the change: Instead of having the standing students share with the class, have the other teams beckon for one of the standing students to join their team. The standing students travel to a new team and remain standing. At the teacher's cue, the standing students share their answer, then sit. The new team celebrates or coaches the traveler. With each question, any student can be randomly selected to travel and share.

Traveling Heads Together can be used for opinion questions. While standing, students discuss an issue and share their opinions on the issue. When the student travels to a new team, he or she can share his or her own opinions or the opinions of others on the issue.

A small variation of Traveling Heads Together that some teachers prefer is to have a preestablished traveling pattern rather than having students beckon for a new teammate. For example, Student #1's move one team ahead; Student #2's move two teams ahead, and so on.

Step 1 Teacher Asks Question

The teacher presents a problem and gives Think Time. (Example: *"Everyone think about why days are shorter in the winter."*)

Step 2 Individuals Write

Students privately write their answers.

Step 3 — Heads Together

Students lift up from their chairs to put their heads together, show answers, and discuss and teach each other.

Step 4 — Students Sit

Students sit down when everyone knows the answer or has something to share.

Step 5 — Teacher Calls a Number

The teacher calls a number. One student on each team with the selected number stands. For example, the teacher calls Student #3 and all Student #3's stand.

Step 6 — Teams Beckon a Classmate

The teacher instructs the seated students to beckon for one of the standing students to join their team.

Step 7 — Traveler Joins Team

Traveling students move to a new team, standing behind the chair of the student who just left, and wait for a cue from the teacher to begin sharing.

Step 8 — Standing Students Share

The teacher gives a cue for the standing students to share their answers, and tells them to sit when they have finished.

Step 9 — Coach or Praise

Seated students coach or praise the traveler.

The Beckoning

To make Traveling Heads Together fun for students, encourage them to "beckon wildly" in Step 6. Students cheer and wave at their traveling classmates. They call, "*Hey Kim, come join us!*" This adds an element of fun, and who doesn't want to feel wanted?

 **ANIMAL FUN FACTS**
Numbered Heads Together

Instructions. Use these fun questions to introduce students to the structure or to play for classbuilding fun.

1 What animals hold hands when they sleep to keep them from drifting apart?

A. walruses C. polar bears
B. sea otters D. seals

B. sea otters

2 Squirrels plant thousands of trees annually by forgetting where they put their acorns. True or False?

true

3 Can any animal breathe through its rear end? Which?

yes, turtles

4 Some spiders can fly. True or false?

false

5 Which insect can taste with its feet?

A. bee C. butterfly
B. ant D. fly

C. butterfly

6 Can an ostrich run as fast as a horse? Yes or No?

yes

7 What animal has four stomachs?

A. horse C. cow
B. goat D. sheep

C. cow

8 How much of our DNA do we share with a chimpanzee?

A. 25–50% C. 75–90%
B. 50–75% D. over 95%

D. over 95%

9 What is the only mammal that can fly?

bat

10 Are ligers and tigons—a cross between tiger and lion—real?

yes, tigon—male tiger breeds with a female lion; liger—male lion breeds with a female tiger.

Structure #18

PAIR SHARE

Structure #18
PAIR SHARE

Partners take turns sharing and listening.

PAIR SHARE is a quick and easy way to get full student engagement. At any point in the lesson, the teacher has students turn to a partner and do a two-way share. Pairs can be face partners, shoulder partners, or even classmates paring up from a StandUp–HandUp–PairUp. There is no end to what students can share. They can share an idea, an answer, an opinion, their feelings, or a solution. The idea with Pair Share is a quick two-way share and to move on. If the response is an elaborated response, a Timed Pair Share is more appropriate. Use Pair Share any time you want every student to participate. It's a great tool to keep everyone tuned in, and it only takes a minute.

Pair Share is in contrast to a Pair Discussion or Turn-N-Talk. In those structures, the high achiever in each pair is likely to do most or even all the talking. In Pair Share, students both share equally. To equalize participation, the teacher might limit the sharing to a few sentences each. For example, the teacher might say, "*Think about the moral of the story. Now summarize your thinking in one sentence that begins with 'the moral is…' Now share your sentences with your partner both ways and then raise a hand to signal you are finished.*"

TRAVELING PAIR SHARE

Traveling Pair Share is a great structure to use during the share time when you want students to briefly share with multiple classmates. For example, "*When I say, 'Go!' I want you to stand up, put a hand up, and pair with a partner. Briefly share one thing that happened in the story. Then find a new partner to share another story event. Keep pairing up until I call, 'Times Up!' Ready, Go!*"

Pair Share vs. Timed Pair Share

There are two key differences between Pair Share and Timed Pair Share. First, in Timed Pair Share, responses are timed so that students have equal share time. This is ideal to create equal participation for elaborate responses. Second, in Timed Pair Share, students respond to each other. Pair Share is for that quick two-way share.

Step 1
Teacher Announces Topic

The teacher announces the topic partners will share about and provides Think Time.

Step 2
First Partner Shares

The teacher selects a partner to begin sharing. The teacher can say, "*Partner A begin,*" or pick a partner using a cue such as, "*Taller partner begin.*" The selected partner shares while his or her partner listens.

Step 3
Second Partner Shares

When the first partner is done sharing, the other partner shares while his or her partner listens.

Step 4
Signal When Finished

Students both raise a hand to signal they have both shared.

Pair Share

WHO STARTS
Pair Share

Teacher Instructions. Use these cues to inform students who shares first. For example, *"The partner with the longer hair shares first."* Mix it up for fun and variety. If partners tie, have a default rule such as tallest partner starts.

PHYSICAL CHARACTERISTICS

Be careful not to use sensitive characteristics such as weight.

- Bigger hand
- Smaller hand
- Taller partner
- Shorter partner
- Partner with head closest to ceiling

- Bigger foot
- Smaller foot
- Longer pinky
- Shorter thumb
- Darker eyes

- Lighter eyes
- Longer hair
- Shorter hair
- Darker hair
- Lighter hair

CLOTHING

Be careful not to use judgement calls such as cuter outfit.

- More buttons
- Fewer buttons
- Darker shirt
- Lighter shirt
- Bigger shoes
- Smaller shoes

- Brighter colors
- More colors
- Fewer colors
- Warmer clothes
- Higher socks
- Lower socks

ABOUT ME

These take more time, but add a little fun, so use accordingly.

- First name comes first alphabetically
- First name comes last alphabetically
- Last name comes first alphabetically
- Last name comes last alphabetically
- Birthday first in the year
- Birthday last in the year

- Number of syllables in favorite band
- Farthest I've traveled
- Bigger favorite animal
- Smaller favorite animal
- Favorite sport alphabetically
- Later bedtime
- Earlier bedtime

- Time of favorite TV show
- Woke up earlier today
- More siblings
- Fewer siblings
- More pets
- Fewer pets

PARAPHRASE PASSPORT

Structure #19
PARAPHRASE PASSPORT

Students earn a passport to speak by accurately paraphrasing the prior speaker. Paraphrase Passport promotes active listening.

STEPS Getting Ready
The teacher prepares the discussion topic.

Step 1
Teacher Assigns Topic

The teacher assigns an open-ended discussion topic. For example, "*What are your feelings about the law?*" Or, "*What do you think might happen next in the story?*" Or, "*Should growing human organs in a lab from human cells be legal?*"

Step 2
One Person Shares

One person in the pair or team shares an idea.

- Very young students can be taught to repeat what their partner has said as a precursor to paraphrasing.
- Start with practicing just one gambit. For example, tell students to use, "*I heard you say… .*" As students improve their paraphrasing skills, provide more sentence starters.

Step 3 — Paraphrase and Check

Any student can share his or her idea next, but first he or she must paraphrase the person who spoke immediately before, checking for accuracy before sharing his or her own idea. "*You think it's a terrific idea for scientists to grow organs from patients' own cells because it will save lives and improve quality of life. Did I hear you right?*"

Step 4 — Offer Passport or Rephrase

If the student who was paraphrased feels the paraphrase accurately reflected his or her thoughts, the student offers the passport for the paraphraser to speak. "*You understood my thinking.*" If the paraphrased student does not feel the paraphrase was accurate, the student takes responsibility, saying, "*I don't think I got my idea across. Let me try again.*" After hearing the idea rephrased by the speaker, the person paraphrasing has another opportunity to earn the passport to speak.

Paraphrase Passport

STRUCTURE POWER

Paraphrase Passport is the royal road to developing social skills and empathy, two dimensions of emotional intelligence. All social skills spring from sensitivity to the needs, feelings, and thoughts of others. Making it a habit to "seek to understand" predicts job, family, and life success. Regardless of the content, when students practice Paraphrase Passport they are acquiring one, if not the most important, social skill—understanding others. Paraphrase Passport holds students accountable for listening. It is in contrast to unstructured discussions in which many are not focused on the speaker but rather on what they want to say next. In the process of focused listening, students develop empathy. Empathy is what produces bonding, friendship, and leadership skills. The skillful leader leads based on understanding the position of others. Empathy is what leads to caring, sharing, and cooperation, as well as the desire not to harm others. Through Paraphrase Passport, students receive feedback on how well they understand others; they develop their mirror neurons. Paraphrase Passport develops that part of the brain associated with not just understanding others, but also the ability to learn from others. Our mirror neurons allow us to learn as we watch others.

TIPS

• **Using Paraphrase Passport with Other Structures**. Paraphrase Passport can be used with other discussion structures such as:
  • Timed Pair Share
  • RallyRobin
  • RoundRobin
  • Agree-Disagree Line-Ups

• **Provide Gambits.** Provide students with sentence starters such as, "*If I heard you correctly… .*" The sentence starters may be posted in the class, or each student may have chips or tokens to use.

• **Students Brainstorm Paraphrasing Gambits.** Use Jot Thoughts or another brainstorming structure to have students brainstorm paraphrase gambits. Post the best gambits.

• **Microphone.** While listening, young students may hold either an imaginary or mock microphone to help them focus on the speaker. Teachers have students make mock microphones by painting the cardboard cylinder inside a paper towel roll and then gluing a ball to one end.

IDEAS Across the Curriculum

Mathematics

Students discuss...
- How to solve a problem
- Ways to use math in everyday living

Language Arts

Students discuss...
- Favorite stories
- Character's motivation
- Story or book read
- Passage
- Story element questions
- Prewriting questions
- Poetry questions

Social Studies

Students discuss...
- Places you would like to visit, and why
- People that are important in history
- Generation X vs. John-Boy Walton
- Textbook discussion questions

Science

Students discuss...
- Steps in a sequence
- Interpretation of a lab experiment's results
- Water cycle
- Acid rain
- Electricity
- Magnetism
- Extinction
- Energy

Art

Students discuss...
- What did you feel when you heard the piece of music or looked at the artwork?

Classbuilding

Students discuss...
- What do you like best about our class?
- What things would you like to change about this class?

PASSPORT STAMP

The teammate who spoke has the stamp. After a teammate paraphrases him or her, that teammate gives the next speaker the stamp to speak. The stamp is passed from teammate to teammate as they receive the passport to speak.

Paraphrase Passport

# PASSPORTS TO SPEAK
Paraphrase Passport

Instructions. Cut out passports and give one to each teammate. Teammates complete a sentence starter on their passport before adding to the discussion.

PASSPORT TO SPEAK

- I heard you say…

- In other words…

- Restating in my own words…

- In summary…

- If I understand…

PASSPORT TO SPEAK

- I heard you say…

- In other words…

- Restating in my own words…

- In summary…

- If I understand…

PASSPORT TO SPEAK

- I heard you say…

- In other words…

- Restating in my own words…

- In summary…

- If I understand…

PASSPORT TO SPEAK

- I heard you say…

- In other words…

- Restating in my own words…

- In summary…

- If I understand…

59 Kagan Structures
Kagan Publishing • 1 (800) 933-2667 • KaganOnline.com

QUIZ-QUIZ-TRADE

Structure #20
QUIZ-QUIZ-TRADE

Students quiz a partner, get quizzed by a partner, and then trade cards to repeat the process with a new partner.

TO PLAY QUIZ-QUIZ-TRADE, each student receives one card. The card has a question or problem on it. For example, when working on countries and capital cities, the card may read "Russia." For times tables, it may read "7 x 8." With cards in hand, students stand up with a hand up and high five to pair up with a partner. Partner A uses the card to quiz the other partner. For example, "*I have Russia. What's the capital city?*" Or, "*What is 7 times 8?*" Partner B answers. If correct, Partner A offers praise: "*That's right. It is Moscow!*" If incorrect, Partner A coaches. If it's a problem to solve, Partner A works it out, discussing it aloud. Next, partners switch roles and quiz the other way. After they have quizzed both ways, they trade cards and find a new partner to quiz, get quizzed, and trade again.

Quiz-Quiz-Trade is a great way to master content knowledge. It makes redundant quizzing an energizing and engaging event, contributing to a positive classroom climate. Quiz-Quiz-Trade is a student favorite as they love interacting with all their classmates.

DIFFERENTIATED INSTRUCTION

Two different sets of question cards may be made, differentiated by content or difficulty. The cards are color-coded, and students are instructed to pair up with others who have the same color.

BENEFITS

Students...

...repeatedly quiz each other.

...enjoy playing, thereby, enhancing the class tone.

...interact with many classmates.

...make connections with partners.

...practice coaching each other.

...develop praising skills.

Step 1 — Students Pair Up

With a card in one hand and the other hand raised, each student stands up, puts a hand up, and pairs up with a classmate. They give each other a high five as they pair up. *"Alright everyone, stand up, hand up, pair up. High five when you pair up and lower your hands so that everyone can quickly find a partner with a hand up."*

Step 2 — Partner A Quizzes

In the pair, Partner A asks Partner B a question relating to his or her card. For example, *"My card says 'Jump'. What part of speech is 'Jump'?"*

Step 3 — Partner B Answers

Partner B answers Partner A's question. *"'Jump' is a verb."*

continued

Quiz-Quiz-Trade

Step 4 Partner A Praises or Coaches

If Partner B answers correctly, Partner A praises him or her. If Partner B answers incorrectly, Partner A coaches or tutors Partner B (see Coaching Tips on page 114).

Step 5 Switch Roles

Partners switch roles. Partner B now asks the question on his or her card and offers praise or coaches.

Step 6 Partners Trade Cards

Before departing and looking for new partners, partners trade cards. This way, students have a new card for each new pairing.

Partners Continue Quizzing and Trading

Partners split up and continue quizzing and getting quizzed by new partners. When done, they trade cards again and find a new partner. Remind students, *"Hand up to find a partner, high five, and hands down when you have a partner."*

Quiz-Quiz-Trade vs. Mix-N-Match

Mix-N-Match is Quiz-Quiz-Trade with a twist. The cards in Mix-N-Match each match another card. For example, when playing Mix-N-Match on states and capitals, there is a matching capital card for each state (California and Sacramento). Mix-N-Match starts with a round of Quiz-Quiz-Trade. After quizzing for the desired period, the teacher tells students to find the classmate with the matching card.

Quiz-Quiz-Trade

STRUCTURE POWER

Traditional worksheet drill and practice is boring. The same content taught with Quiz-Quiz-Trade becomes an exciting, energizing game! Students want to move, and they want to talk with each other. In the traditional classroom, we tell them, "*Sit down and don't talk.*" We are going against students' basic impulses. And it turns out their impulses are right, and traditional worksheet work is wrong. When students move, they have more oxygen and glucose in the brain. And when they talk, their brains get more fully engaged. With Quiz-Quiz-Trade, students move and talk, but we channel that energy into learning. It is win-win. Students get to do what they most want while we get what we most want—student learning!

TIPS

• **Coaching Tips.** Here are two effective coaching strategies you can use with Quiz-Quiz-Trade:

1. Tip, Tip, Teach, Try Again. The coach provides one tip, and then asks the question again. If still incorrect, the coach provides a second tip, and then reasks the question. If still incorrect, the coach instructs and then reasks the question. The coach praises his or her partner when the partner answers correctly.

2. Tell and Teach. The coach provides the answer and teaches his or her partner how to reach or remember the answer.

• **Tips on Cards.** The quizzing cards can have two tips. If a student answers incorrectly or asks for a tip, the quizzing student provides a tip from the card.

• **Student Cards.** Have students make their own quizzing cards. The cards have the question on the front and the answer on the back (3" x 5" index cards work well). Have students submit the cards first for the teacher to review for accuracy.

• **Model It.** Before playing for the first time, the teacher selects a student and models the Quiz-Quiz-Trade process for the class.

• **Hand Up.** Be sure to enforce the Hand Up Rule. This makes it quick and easy for students to tell who needs a partner. Students give a high five to pair up then lower their hands.

• **Move Out.** For management, you may have students move to the center of the room when looking for a partner and have pairs move out from the center of the room while quizzing each other.

IDEAS Across the Curriculum

Mathematics
- Matching patterns
- Clocks: digital and analog
- Geometric shapes and names
- Fractions and equivalents
- Measurements and conversions
- Fractions and percents
- Coins and values
- Patterns—what comes next
- Telling time
- Multiplication facts

Language Arts
- Proper nouns/common nouns
- Synonyms and antonyms
- Spelling word and definition
- Uppercase and lowercase (A = a)
- Cause and effect
- Compound words
- Initial letter identification
- Story elements
- How did you feel when…
- Fact/opinion

Social Studies
- States and capitals
- Colonies and founders
- Continents and names
- Famous athlete
- Famous people: quotes
- Famous people: known for
- Geography term and definition
- Map reading skills
- Bill of Rights
- Important events—Treaty of Paris
- Rules

Science
- Color and color words
- Vocabulary word and definition
- Animals and babies
- Animals and species
- Elements and symbols
- Inventors and inventions
- Microscope and parts
- Parts of plants
- Conservation questions

Music
- Jingles and slogans
- Instrument and name
- Identify instruments
- Musical notes
- Read notes—name that tune
- Clap this pattern
- Singers and songs
- Pictures and words
- Practice greetings

Art
- Art and artist
- Famous artwork/artists
- What time period is this painting from?
- What is the artist trying to convey?
- Identify art tools

Classbuilding
- Students' names and pictures
- Singers and songs
- Disney characters and story
- Slogans:"Just Do It" = Nike
- Favorites
- About you
- Vacations

Second Language
- Picture and vocabulary word
- English and foreign word
- Holiday

Quiz-Quiz-Trade

RELATED STRUCTURES

#21 Quiz-N-Compare

In Quiz-N-Compare, students complete worksheets by pairing up with multiple partners and comparing answers. To play, students stand up, hand up, and pair up, each with their own worksheet. In pairs, Partner A asks the first question on the worksheet. Partner B answers. Partner A praises or coaches. They record the answer when they reach consensus. Then they switch roles, and Partner B asks the second question. Both partners check off the questions they've covered, then give each other a high five before they find a new partner to answer more questions.

Step 1 Students Pair Up

Each student has a worksheet and a pen or pencil. They stand up, put a hand up, and pair up with a nearby classmate.

Step 2 Partner A Asks

In the pair, Partner A asks Partner B a question on the worksheet.

Step 3 Partner B Responds

Partner B responds. If Partner A agrees, they celebrate; if Partner A disagrees, Partner A coaches or they solve it together.

Step 4 Record Answer

When both partners agree, they both record the answer on their own worksheets.

Step 5 Switch Roles

Partner B now asks the question, and Partner A responds. When they reach consensus, they both record the answer.

Step 6 Find a New Partner

Students thank each other, put a hand up, and pair up with a new partner to solve the next problem on their worksheet. After solving all the problems, students can check their answers with new partners, reaching consensus where they have different answers.

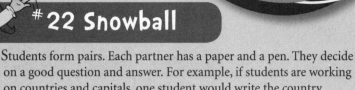

#22 Snowball

Students form pairs. Each partner has a paper and a pen. They decide on a good question and answer. For example, if students are working on countries and capitals, one student would write the country name on his or her sheet (*France*), and the other would write the capital of that country on his or her sheet (*Paris*). In a chemistry class, one student might write, "*What is the symbol for salt?*" and the other would write, "*NaCl.*" Students with the questions move to one side of the classroom (or if played outside, one side of a line chalked on the ground), and students with the answers move to the other side.

Students then crumple their papers. At a signal from the teacher, students have a friendly snowball fight. The goal is to have as few snowballs on your side as possible when the teacher calls, "*Stop!*" Students then each pick up one snowball. When each student has one snowball, the teacher calls, "*Go!*" At this signal, students with questions rush to find the student holding the question or answer that matches their card.

After a few rounds, Snowball can be used to form random teams. Two matching pairs pair up to form a team of four.

 ## Students Pair Up

Students form pairs, each with a sheet of paper. They decide on a good question and answer.

 ## Students Write

One partner writes the question on one sheet. The other partner writes the answer on the other sheet.

 ## Students Line Up

All Partner A's go to one side of the classroom. Partner B's go to the other side.

 ## Snowball Fight!

The teacher instructs students to crumple up their papers into a snowball. They throw the snowball to the other side of the room (not at anyone!). Their goal is to keep all the snowballs on the opposite side of the room. After a brief, friendly fight, each student collects one snowball.

 ## Find Partner

The teacher calls, "*Go!*" and students rush to find the classmate who has the matching question or answer.

Tip:

Make it easy to determine if a sheet has a question or answer. This is helpful for finding a partner. These are a few easy ways to do this. One way is to write a large "Q" or "A" on the sheet, representing either "Question" or "Answer." Another way is to have all Partner As write the question in black and Partner Bs write the answer in red. Another way is to write questions and answers on different colored papers.

Timed Pair Share

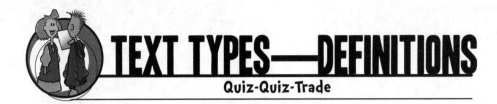

Instructions: These are sample Text Type quiz cards. To play, each student receives a card to quiz a partner.

Text Types—Definitions	Text Types—Definitions
Question: Which text type **tells a story?**	**Answer:** narrative
Question: Which text type **gives facts and information?**	**Answer:** expository
Question: Which text type **gives information needed to perform a task?**	**Answer:** technical
Question: Which text type **tries to convince the reader?**	**Answer:** persuasive

SOURCE: Skidmore, S. & Graber, J. *Balanced Literacy Grade 5*. San Clemente, CA: Kagan Publishing.

ARRAYS
Quiz-Quiz-Trade

Instructions. These are sample Arrays quiz cards. To play, each student receives a card to quiz a partner.

13 Question — Arrays	**13** Answer — Arrays **3 x 1 =**
14 Question — Arrays	**14** Answer — Arrays **3 x 2 =**
15 Question — Arrays	**15** Answer — Arrays **3 x 3 =**
16 Question — Arrays	**16** Answer — Arrays **3 x 4 =**

SOURCE: Stites. R & Pfannenstiel, A. *Cooperative Math Grades 3–5*. San Clemente, CA: Kagan Publishing.

COUNTING COINS
Quiz-Quiz-Trade

Instructions. These are sample Counting Coins quiz cards. To play, each student receives a card to quiz a partner.

59 Kagan Structures
Kagan Publishing • 1 (800) 933-2667 • KaganOnline.com

MOLE CONVERSIONS

Quiz-Quiz-Trade

Instructions. These are sample Mole Conversions quiz cards. To play, each student receives a card to quiz a partner.

9 — Mole Conversions

How many mol are there in 11.2 L of neon at STP?

ANSWER: 11.2/22.4 = 0.5 mol

10 — Mole Conversions

What is the volume at STP of 0.1 mol of helium?

ANSWER: 0.1 x 22.4 = 2.24 L

11 — Mole Conversions

How many mol are there in 44.8 L of nitrogen at STP?

ANSWER: 44.8/22.4 = 2 mol

12 — Mole Conversions

What is the volume at STP of 2 mol of sulferdioxide?

ANSWER: 2 x 22.4 = 44.8 L

13 — Mole Conversions

How many mol are there in 224 L of krypton at STP?

ANSWER: 224/22.4 = 10 mol

14 — Mole Conversions

What is the volume at STP of 10 mol of xenon?

ANSWER: 10 x 22.4 = 224 L

15 — Mole Conversions

How many mol are there in 12 x 10^{23} molecules of Argon?

ANSWER: 12 x 10^{23}/6 x 10^{23} = 2 mol

16 — Mole Conversions

What is the number of molecules in 3 mol of F_2?

ANSWER: 3 x 6 x 10^{23} = 18 x 10^{23} molecules

SOURCE: Plumb, D. *Structures for Success in Chemistry*. San Clemente, CA: Kagan Publishing.

TEMPO TERMS
Quiz-Quiz-Trade

Instructions. These are sample Tempo Terms quiz cards for music terms. To play, each student receives a card to quiz a partner.

Tempo Terms 5

How fast is the tempo called "Largo"?

Answer: very slow tempo

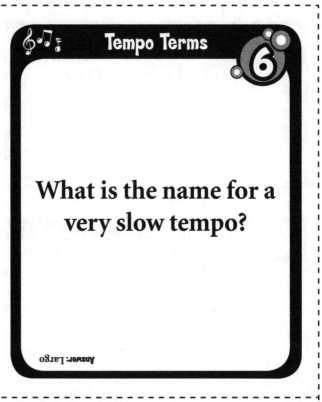

Tempo Terms 6

What is the name for a very slow tempo?

Answer: Largo

Tempo Terms 7

How fast is the tempo called "Lento" (len'-toh)?

Answer: slow tempo

Tempo Terms 8

What is the name for a slow tempo?

Answer: Lento

SOURCE: Katz, M. & Brown, C. *Cooperative Learning & Music*. San Clemente, CA: Kagan Publishing.

RALLYCOACH

Structure #23
RALLYCOACH

In pairs, each student takes a turn solving a problem while the other coaches.

RALLYCOACH promotes peer tutoring during problem solving. Students pair up, usually with their shoulder partners on their own team. The pair receives a set of problems to solve. The problems are typically mastery-oriented practice problems, such as math worksheets or grammar practice. But RallyCoach can also be used with more challenging or creative problems to solve. It is used in welding class, music class, and on the athletic field as students practice new skills. In the pair, usually one student is the Solver and the other is the Coach. The Solver works out the problem, verbalizing the steps as he or she solves it. The Coach watches and listens. The Coach offers help if needed. When the Solver solves the problem, the Coach offers specific praise, "*Great job partner! You used the correct order of operations!*" Partners switch roles and the Solver becomes the Coach for the next problem.

A crucial ingredient to student success is receiving specific and immediate help. While working independently on problem solving, students may get stuck, be unaware of errors they are making, or not know how to solve even the first problem. Working alone, the minds of some students wander. In contrast, RallyCoach structures for immediate help. Each student has a coach, and each is accountable to a partner for staying on task.

DIFFERENTIATED INSTRUCTION

- Homogeneous pairs may be working on developmentally appropriate curriculum.
- An aide or assistant may be a partner.
- Pairs work at their own pace.

BENEFITS

Students...

...verbalize their problem-solving strategies.

...are accountable to their partners for staying on task.

...have coaches as immediate peer-tutoring resources.

...give and receive immediate and specific feedback.

Getting Ready: *The teacher prepares a set of problems. Each pair receives only one pencil or pen and one problem worksheet or a piece of paper to answer the problems.*

Step 1 — Partner A Solves

In shoulder partners, Partner A solves the first problem, verbalizing the steps or procedures aloud.

Step 2 — Partner B Coaches and Praises

Partner B acts as the coach. Partner B watches, listens, and checks. If Partner A gets an incorrect answer or needs help, Partner B coaches. If Partner A solves the problem correctly, Partner B praises.

Step 3 — Partner B Solves

Students switch roles and Partner B now solves the next problem, talking it out.

Step 4 — Partner A Coaches and Praises

Partner A now acts as the coach: watching, listening, checking, coaching, and praising.

Step 5 — Continue Solving

The process is repeated for each new problem.

Note:

If students are practicing a skill like welding or kicking a soccer ball, students take turns, one performing while the other watches and gives feedback and an opportunity to improve if necessary.

RallyCoach

STRUCTURE POWER

A veteran teacher came to me at our Summer Academy and said she was back for a second year of training because of the success she had following the first year. She had taught geometry for 23 years and knew exactly how many chapters she could complete in a semester. Following the first year of Kagan training, she completed three additional chapters in her classes. When I asked how that had happened, she said, "*For 23 years I had been giving the best presentations I could and then assigned homework for students to practice. I diligently graded the homework and then spent about 10 minutes in class the next day going over the problems that the students had missed. After training in Kagan Structures, I used RallyCoach for guided practice, before independent practice, or homework. When I graded their homework, they had the problems correct. We saved almost a full 10 minutes of a class period each day. That added up to three more chapters a semester.*"

RallyCoach is powerful. Students, who would have practiced incorrectly on a worksheet, get immediate correction. During RallyCoach, students receive feedback after every problem, not after every worksheet. In the traditional classroom, when graded homework is passed back, students look around to compare—who is better, who is worse. With RallyCoach, they relate as equals with their fellow students, encouraging and tutoring, hoping their classmates did well. An entirely different social orientation emerges. Instead of "*Who did I beat and who beat me?*" it becomes "*How can I help you?*" Instead of a class where evaluation is the bottom line; it is a class where learning is the ultimate goal.

TIPS

• **Shoulder Partners.** Students work as shoulder partners to help lessen the ability gap. The high- and low-medium students are shoulder partners, and the low- and high-medium students are partners. The benefit of pairing with shoulder partners is that no partner needs to read upside down, as is the case with face partners.

• **Think Aloud.** Model for students what it means to verbalize their thinking as they solve the problem.

• **Fold Worksheet.** RallyCoach worksheets are best when Partner A and Partner B problems are on opposite halves of the paper. That way, they can fold the paper in half and focus on the current problem. See sample worksheets provided (pages 130–132).

• **Consult Teammates.** If the pair gets stuck on a problem or has a question, they can consult the other pair on their team. If the other pair doesn't know, everyone raises a hand indicating to the teacher that they have a team question.

• **Teach Coaching.** Model for students what good coaching looks like and sounds like.

• **Teach Praising.** Have students generate and practice surprising and delightful praisers prior to using RallyCoach.

• **Sponge.** Pairs will finish at different rates, so have challenge problems, more problems, or a sponge activity ready for pairs who finish early.

• **No Grades.** Because there is no way to tell which student did the work, RallyCoach is not graded.

IDEAS Across the Curriculum

Mathematics

- Telling time
- Patterns
- Measurement
- Story problems
- Decimals from words
- Change for a dollar
- Read whole numbers
- Identify congruent figures
- Use correct order of operations
- Simplify fractions
- Apply factoring techniques
- Define geometry terms
- Compute surface areas
- Compute derivatives

Language Arts

- Realism vs. Fantasy
- Spell irregular words correctly
- Write a letter, word, or phrase in cursive
- Identify parts of a letter
- Use correct punctuation
- Respond to questions
- Read for fluency
- Determine word meanings

Social Studies

- Chapter review questions
- Follow directions to make maps
- Place items on a time line
- Identify American symbols
- Describe an amendment
- Locate something on a map
- Identify geographic features
- Describe the importance of a landmark
- Describe the contribution of American heroes

Science

- What does not belong in the group?
- Identify materials items are made of (rubber, plastic, cloth, metal)
- Identify state of matter
- Identify plant structures (stem, leaf, roots)
- Identify animal structures (arm, wing, leg)
- Answer questions about heat and thermodynamics
- Use the periodic table to identify elements
- Convert between Celsius and Kelvin

Music

- Notes/symbols
- Perform a rhythmic pattern
- Identify musical forms (AABA, AABB, round)
- Identify instruments
- Play melodic ostinatos
- Read diatonic scales
- Define music terminology

Art

- Create a pattern
- Mix secondary colors from primary colors
- Convert a 2D shape into a 3D shape
- Identify complementary colors

Second Language

- Vocabulary

RallyCoach

VARIATIONS

- **RallyCoach for Oral Problems.** The teacher gives the class problems orally, and students use RallyCoach to solve the problems.

- **RallyCoach with Manipulatives.** Students use RallyCoach with manipulatives to solve problems.

- **Timed RallyCoach.** For some skills that don't have a definite ending like a golf swing, the student performs for a preset time, receiving ongoing coaching from their partner. When time is up, they switch roles.

RallyCoach Team Setup

In teams, have students work with shoulder partners.

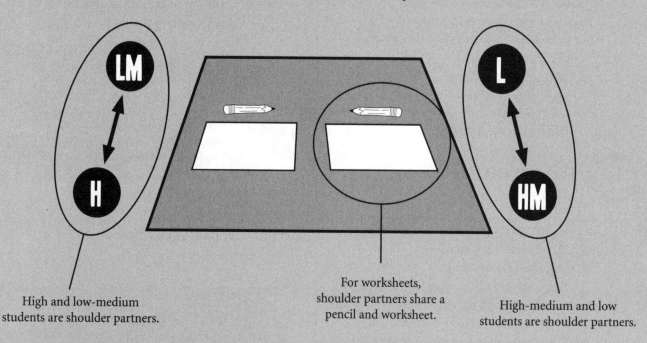

High and low-medium students are shoulder partners.

For worksheets, shoulder partners share a pencil and worksheet.

High-medium and low students are shoulder partners.

Note:

Although the high and low achiever on each team are seated kitty corner to each other, they are not in the same corners in each team to avoid low achieving students being labeled as in the "low corner."

RELATED STRUCTURE

#24 Mix-Pair-RallyCoach

The teacher asks a question or posts a problem on the board. Students mix with a hand up and find a partner. Partner A solves the problem while Partner B coaches. The teacher asks or displays the next question. Partner B now solves the problem and Partner A coaches. After each partner has solved a problem, they mix and pair up with a new partner to do RallyCoach with the next two questions, and so on. For some types of problems, students may carry a clipboard or AnswerBoard to work out the problems.

Step 1 Students Mix

Students "Mix" around the room.

Step 2 Students Pair

The teacher calls, "*Pair*." Students pair up with the nearest classmate.

Step 3 Teacher Asks Question

The teacher poses a question. The teacher can ask it orally, write it on the board, or display it on the screen.

Step 4 Partner A Solves Problem

Partner A solves the problem while Partner B watches, checks, coaches if necessary, and praises.

Step 5 Teacher Asks Question

The teacher poses another question.

Step 6 Partner B Solves Problem

Partner B solves the problem while Partner A watches, checks, coaches if necessary, and praises.

Step 7 Repeat

The teacher tells the class, "*Give your partner a high five. Mix in the class until I call, 'pair.'*" The process repeats with students solving one problem, then serving as the coach on the other.

ADDITION/SUBTRACTION WORD PROBLEMS
RallyCoach

Instructions: Read the word problem, decide which operation to use, and think aloud as you solve the problem.

 Student A _____

1. There were 4,231 CDs in the music store. Then the music store got 1,367 new CDs. What was the total number of CDs in the music store?

_____ **Answer**

2. At the zoo, there were 768 boys and 356 girls. How many more boys were at the zoo than girls?

_____ **Answer**

3. TJ is saving money to buy a birdhouse. The birdhouse costs $357. He'll also need to buy a birdbath for $34. How much money does he need to save?

_____ **Answer**

4. A new movie theater plans to serve 3,000 people in the first week it is open. During the first week, the theater served 1,389 more people than expected. How many people did the theater serve in its first week?

_____ **Answer**

5. A clothing company has 30,000 pairs of shorts to give away at the weekend opening of a new store. The company gave away 14,234 on Friday and 11,987 on Saturday. How many pairs of shorts does the company have left to give away on Sunday?

_____ **Answer**

 Student B _____

1. Taylor borrowed $75 from her brother last week. This week, she paid back $17.35. How much money does Taylor still owe her brother?

_____ **Answer**

2. There were 457 people at the baseball stadium. During the game, 298 more people came. What was the total number of people at the stadium?

_____ **Answer**

3. A bookstore had a two-day book sale. On the first day, 4,234 books were sold. On the second day, 3,234 books were sold. What was the total number of books sold?

_____ **Answer**

4. The number of people who went to a football game on Friday was 7,453. The number of people who went on Saturday was 9,323. How many more people went on Saturday than Friday?

_____ **Answer**

5. A distance between two cities using one route is 708.1 miles. The distance using a different route between the same two cities is 534.2 miles. How much shorter is the second route?

_____ **Answer**

SOURCE: Stites, R. & Pfannenstiel, A. *Cooperative Math Grades 3–5.* San Clemente, CA: Kagan Publishing.

GRAPHS
RallyCoach

Instructions: Analyze each graph and answer the questions. Explain your thinking to your coach.

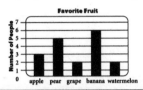

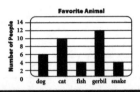

A Student A _____	**B** Student B _____
1. How many students chose apples or grapes? _____	**1.** How many students chose pears or bananas?_____
2. How many more students chose bananas than grapes? _____	**2.** If three more people picked grapes, how many people picked grapes? _____
3. How many students are represented in the fruit graph? _____	**3.** How many more people picked pears than picked grapes? _____
4. If 20 students were surveyed about their favorite fruit, how many students are not represented in the graph? _____	**4.** How many more people picked apples or pears than picked grapes or watermelon? _____
5. What is the title of the fruit graph? _____	**5.** What is the title of the animal graph?_____
6. How many people chose fish or gerbils as their favorite animal? _____	**6.** How many students chose snakes or fish? _____
7. If four more people picked cats, how many people would have picked cats? _____	**7.** How many students are represented in the second graph? _____
8. How many more people picked cats than dogs? _____	**8.** If 50 students chose their favorite animal, how many students are not represented in the graph? _____
9. How many more people picked cats or fish than snakes or dogs? _____	**9.** How many students chose fish or gerbils? _____

SOURCE: Stites, R. & Pfannenstiel, A. *Cooperative Math Grades 3–5*. San Clemente, CA: Kagan Publishing.

CONTRACTIONS
RallyCoach

Instructions. Take turns working with your partner to write the contraction for each pair of words using RallyCoach.

PARTNER A	PARTNER B
Name _____	**Name** _____
1 she is _____	**1** is not _____
2 does not _____	**2** we will _____
3 we would _____	**3** was not _____
4 you have _____	**4** you are _____
5 do not _____	**5** you would _____
6 they would _____	**6** we will _____
7 were not _____	**7** they are _____
8 that is _____	**8** I have _____
9 would not _____	**9** it is _____
10 I am _____	**10** you have _____
11 was not _____	**11** are not _____
12 you will _____	**12** he would _____
13 there is _____	**13** she will _____

SOURCE: Agrew, M. & McCoy, S. *Cooperative Learning & Grammar Grades 3–5.* San Clemente, CA: Kagan Publishing.

RALLYQUIZ

Structure #25
RALLYQUIZ

Students take turns quizzing their partner.

THERE ARE many times we want students to have repeated practice with the curriculum. When the content doesn't require in-depth problem solving, RallyCoach is overkill because there is no need for students to talk through their thinking and solve detailed problems. Memorizing multiplication facts is a good example. For repeated practice, quizzing works well. RallyQuiz is a great structure to have students pair up and quiz each other. Partners take turns asking each other the next question. Quizzing with a partner is more fun for students than going it alone. RallyQuiz can also be used with thinking questions where students take turns asking each other questions and responding.

IDEAS Across the Curriculum

Mathematics
• What is 7 x 8?
• What is the name of a shape with eight sides?
• What is the formula for the area of a triangle?

Language Arts
• How do you spell *personification*?
• What was the setting of the story?
• Which word is correct for the sentence, *bare* or *bear*?

Social Studies
• What are the three branches of government?
• What is Gandhi famous for?
• What were the Jim Crow laws?

Science
• What are the three states of matter?
• Where is the magma chamber on the volcano diagram?
• What is the role of the mitochondria?

Step 1 — Partner A Quizzes

Partner A asks Partner B the first question on the list. The question can be a review question, "*Who said, 'To be or not to be…'?*" The question can also be a thinking question such as, "*What issue does the question, 'To be or not to be…' deal with?*"

Step 2 — Partner B Answers

Partner B answers. For a quiz question, Partner B simply states the answer. "*Prince Hamlet said it.*" For a thinking question, Partner B shares an elaborated response. "*Hamlet is contemplating suicide and is grappling with the meaning of life and death.*"

Step 3 — Partner A Praises

For thought questions: A praises the thinking. For review questions: A checks for correctness. If Partner B answered correctly, Partner A validates the answer. If not correct, Partner A gives the answer, re-asks the question, then praises the correct answer. If not, A coaches, re-asks, then praises.

Step 4 — Students Switch

Students switch roles so that Partner B now quizzes Partner A. Students alternate asking and answering each question.

RallyQuiz

RELATED STRUCTURES

#26 Traveling RallyQuiz

Students StandUp–HandUp–PairUp to find a partner who is not a teammate. Partner A asks Partner B one of the questions on his or her list. Partner B answers. For thinking questions, Partner A praises the thinking; for review questions, Partner A praises if the answer is correct, or coaches if the answer is incorrect. Students switch roles so that Partner B quizzes, then praises or coaches. Students check off the question they have asked. Students give each other a pat on the back, raise a hand, and seek a new classmate to partner with, repeating the process using a new question from their list.

Students Create List

In teams, students use AllRecord Consensus to generate a list of review and/or thought questions on the topic. The result is each student will have his or her own list of questions on a sheet of paper.

Pair Up

Students take their sheet of questions and a pen, stand up, put a hand up, and pair up with a classmate.

Partner A Asks Question

Partner A asks Partner B a question from his or her list.

Partner B Answers

Partner B answers the question.

Partner A Praises or Coaches

For thought questions, Partner A praises the thinking. For review questions, Partner A checks the answer. If the answer is correct, Partner A praises Partner B. If the answer is incorrect, Partner A coaches, re-asks the question, then praises the correct answer.

Switch Roles

Students switch roles so that Partner B now quizzes Partner A, then praises or coaches.

Students Find New Partners

Students give each other a pat on the back, raise a hand, and seek a new classmate to partner with, repeating the process using a new question from their list.

RALLYROBIN

Structure #27
RALLYROBIN

In pairs, students take turns generating oral responses.

STEPS

Step 1 · Teacher Announces a Topic

The teacher poses a problem to which there are multiple possible responses or solutions. For example, "*How many ways can you make one dollar with coins?*" Or, "*Come up with some metaphors.*"

Step 2 · Partners Take Turns

In pairs, students take turns orally stating responses or solutions. For example:

- Partner A: "*Four quarters.*"
- Partner B: "*Two quarters and five dimes.*"
- Partner A: "*One dollar coin.*"
- Partner B: "*Two half-dollar coins.*"

BENEFITS

Students...

...are actively engaged either sharing or listening.

...regularly express themselves.

...must participate.

...take turns.

...practice respectful listening.

...actively listen so that they may respond appropriately.

...hear classmates' thoughts on the content or issues.

...remember the content more by verbalizing answers.

59 Kagan Structures
Kagan Publishing • 1 (800) 933-2667 • KaganOnline.com

RELATED STRUCTURES

#28 Both Record RallyRobin

Both partners record on their own papers each idea stated in the RallyRobin. This structure engages both students the entire time and results in each student having his or her own sheet, which can be used for independent writing, sharing with a classmate, or quizzing a classmate.

Teacher Asks a Question

The teacher poses a problem to which there are multiple possible responses or solutions.

Students Respond and Record

In pairs, students take turns stating responses or solutions, each recording each answer on their own paper.

#29 RallyInterview

Partners take turns asking each other questions about the topic and receiving a response.

Teacher Assigns Topic

The teacher poses interview questions, or students create interview questions.

Students Interview

In pairs, students take turns interviewing their partners on each question.

#30 RallyRead

Partners take turns reading aloud. After reading for a specified time or amount (either a sentence, paragraph, page, or for a time limit), partners switch roles.

 Teacher Assigns Reading

The teacher provides reading material and states how much or how long each student should read to his or her partner. For example, it may be for 1 minute or 1 page.

 Partner A Reads to B

Partner A now reads to Partner B for the specified time or amount.

 Partner B Reads to A

Partner B reads to Partner A for the specified time or amount.

 Repeat

Partners continue taking turns reading.

#31 RallyRecall

RallyRecall is a RallyRobin specifically for recall. Students take turns stating information that has been presented. RallyRecall is most often used at various intervals during a lecture, reading, or video. Taking the time to process the content periodically makes it more memorable. RallyRecall can also be used for a review at the end of the day, the next day as a memory jogger, or before a test as a review. For example, *"What do you remember about Mother Teresa?"*

 Teacher Reads

The teacher reads a portion of a story or text, or presents a portion of a lecture, then stops.

 Students RallyRobin

In pairs, students do a RallyRobin, taking turns describing key points they recall.

 Teacher Reinforces Points

The teacher reinforces key points and resumes the presentation.

 Pairs Celebrate

Pairs celebrate if they described the key points the teacher shared.

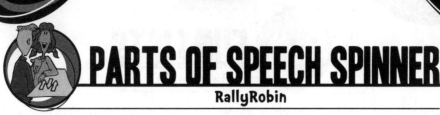

PARTS OF SPEECH SPINNER

RallyRobin

Instructions. In pairs, take turns spinning the spinner and stating a word matching the part of speech the spinner selects.

Preposition

Noun

Pronoun

Verb

Adjective

FUN LISTS
RallyRobin

Teacher Instructions. Use one or more of the following topics to have students RallyRobin examples. These fun topics are great for teaching RallyRobin or can be used at any time for teambuilding.

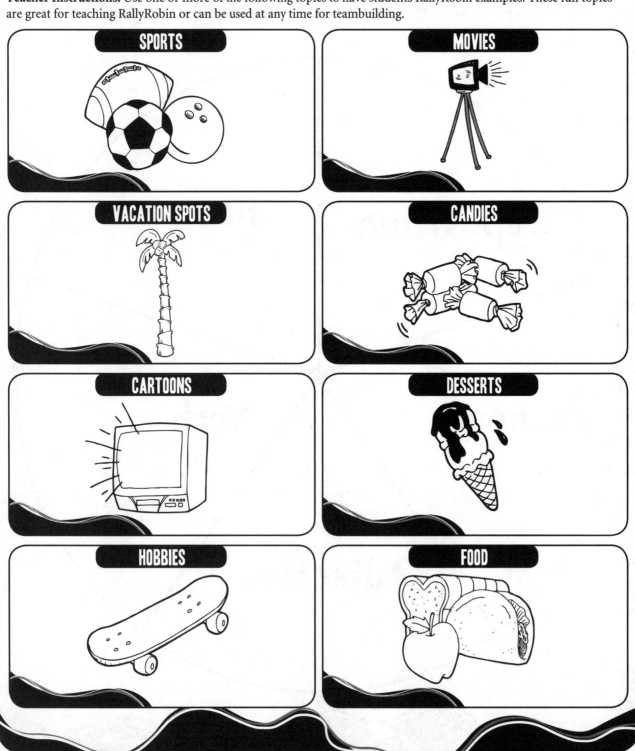

Structure #32

RALLYTABLE

Structure #32
RALLYTABLE

In pairs, students take turns generating written responses or making contributions to a project.

STEPS **Getting Ready:** *Each pair receives one paper and one pencil or pen to record responses. Or, pairs receive materials to build the pair project.*

Step 1 — Teacher Assigns a Task

The teacher provides a task. The task can be a question to which there are multiple possible responses. For example, *"What are some examples of the uses of pliers?"* Or, the task can be a pair project. For example, *"As a pair, you are to build a collage to represent your selected animal."*

Step 2 — Partners Take Turns

In pairs, students take turns. For written responses, partners pass the paper and pencil, each in turn writing one answer. For a project, each partner takes a turn making a contribution.

· **Shoulder Partners.** Students pair up with their shoulder partners so that they are seated side by side.

· **Think Aloud.** As students make their contributions, have them verbalize their thinking to their partners.

· **Color Code.** Give each partner a different colored pen or marker. As you monitor, you can see they are taking turns and who has written each response.

IDEAS Across the Curriculum

Mathematics

Generate a list of…
• Numbers that add up to 100
• Even numbers
• Math uses in the real world
• Objects with a triangular shape
• Jobs that require mathematics

Language Arts

• Plot story on time line
• How would the story be different if…?
• Alphabetize a list

Generate a list of…
• Events in the story
• Nouns/verbs/adjectives
• Words with double letters
• Exclamations
• Adjectives to describe the setting
• Grammar rules

Social Studies

Generate a list of…
• What events led up to the war?
• Famous Americans
• Benefits of mass production
• Drawbacks of child labor
• Characteristics of Pilgrims
• States and their capitals
• Disasters
• Countries
• Wars
• Holidays

Science

• List living things
• What do you know about the solar system?

Generate a list of…
• Possible outcomes to an experiment
• Science fair ideas
• Elements
• Things I remember about the lesson
• What a magnet will stick to
• Things that float
• Uses of technology
• Bones in the body

Music

• List musical instruments

Teambuilding and Classbuilding

Generate a list of…
• Possible team/class names
• Possible team logos
• Party theme ideas
• Qualities of a good teammate
• Jobs that require cooperation
• Things to say to encourage a teammate
• Ideas to get to know classmates better
• Hobbies I like
• Favorite food
• TV shows I watch
• Games I like to play

Second Language

• People in the community

RallyTable

VARIATIONS

- **Pass-N-Praise.** Students praise their partners' contributions each time the paper or the project is passed to them.

- **Timed Turns.** When students may take long or uneven turns, use a timer. Set the timer for 1 minute, so each minute partners switch off who is making the contribution to the pair project.

RELATED STRUCTURES

#33 RallyTable Consensus

Students must get approval from their partner before they write the next response or make the next contribution to the pair project. If an answer or idea is rejected, the pair discusses options and tries to reach consensus.

Step 1 Teacher Assigns a Task

The teacher assigns the pair a list or project. For example, "*List products of the rain forest.*"

Step 2 Partner Proposes Idea

The partner whose turn it is proposes an idea to add to the list or project. For example, "*Rubber is a product of the rain forest. Do you agree?*"

Step 3 Consensus

If partners agree, the student who proposed the idea writes it down. If a partner disagrees, they hash it out until they reach consensus, then record it. If they can't reach consensus, they either move on to a different idea or get help from the neighboring pair or from the teacher.

Step 4 Switch Roles

Partners switch roles for each new item. They propose it, reach consensus, record it, and switch roles.

#34 Simultaneous RallyTable

Pairs have two pieces of paper and two pencils. They each write at the same time, then trade at the same time. Students review their partners' last contribution before adding to the list, drawing, or story. Different colored pens or markers allow accountability for contributions. For example, one student may be adding an item to a list of mammals while the other student is adding to a list of amphibians, and then they trade lists to continue adding items.

Step 1 Teacher Assigns Topic

The teacher assigns either the same topics for each partner, or a different topic for each. For worksheet work, the teacher either assigns both partners the same worksheet or each has a different worksheet.

Step 2 Students Label Paper

If there are two topics, one student labels a paper with one topic while the other student labels the other paper with the other topic. If there is one topic, each student labels his or her paper with the same topic.

Step 3 Students Record Response

Each student records a response on his or her sheet.

Step 4 Students Exchange Papers

Students exchange papers to record each new question or idea.
- For lists, each student adds another item to the list.
- For worksheets, each does the next problem.
- For drawings, each adds something to the drawing they receive.

SAMPLE CONTENT		
	List 1	List 2
Math	Things that have a right angle	Things that have a circle
Science	Plants	Animals
Language Arts	Sentences with adjectives	Sentences with adverbs
Social Studies	Functions of executive branch	Functions of legislative branch

RALLYTABLE REVIEW

RallyTable

Instructions. Take turns listing information you recall from the lesson, lecture, video, story, or chapter.

PARTNER A	PARTNER B
①	②
③	④
⑤	⑥
⑦	⑧
⑨	⑩
⑪	⑫

Structure # 35

READ-N-REVIEW

Structure #35
READ-N-REVIEW

Partners take turns reading passages and quizzing each other to enhance attention and comprehension.

STEPS

Getting Ready
Students pair up. The teacher tells the class how much or how long students are to read before they quiz their partner: after every 3 minutes (or selected time), after every paragraph, after every page, or after every section.

Step 1 Partner A Reads

Partner A reads aloud the assigned section (or for the allotted time) while Partner B listens.

Step 2 Partner A Asks Review Questions

Partner A asks Partner B one or more comprehension questions about what he or she just read. For example, "*Where did the main character go?*" Or, "*What was the magnitude of the earthquake?*" Or, "*What was the scientist's hypothesis?*"

Step 3 Partner B Responds

Partner B responds to the review question(s).

Step 4: Partner A Praises or Coaches

If Partner B answers correctly, Partner A praises. If Partner B answers incorrectly, Partner A provides the correct answer, referring Partner B to the appropriate part of the text.

Step 5: Switch Roles

Partners switch roles, taking turns reading and quizzing each other on their assigned readings.

DINOSAUR FACTS
Read-N-Review

Instructions. Read the following in pairs. Partner A reads two sentences, then asks Partner B a question about the reading. Partner B answers. Partner A praises or coaches. Switch roles after every two sentences.

Dinosaurs lived long, long ago. They first appeared on Earth over 200 million years ago. **STOP** Today, dinosaurs are extinct. Extinct means they have died out and no longer live on Earth. **STOP** Fossil records indicate that birds evolved from a type of dinosaur. Birds survived the extinction event that occurred 66 million years ago. **STOP**

Scientists who study dinosaurs are called paleontologists. They have learned much about what we know about dinosaurs from fossils, bones, and remains dinosaurs left on Earth. **STOP** There are over 1,000 different species of dinosaurs. There are fossil remains of dinosaurs on every continent. **STOP** Some dinosaurs, called carnivores, ate meat, and some dinosaurs, called herbivores, ate plants. The biggest dinosaurs were herbivores. **STOP** The word *dinosaur* means "terrible lizard." Terrible means "terribly large," not mean or bad. **STOP** The largest dinosaurs were as long as 100 feet and had a height of 30 feet. This is bigger than most houses! **STOP**

59 Kagan Structures
Kagan Publishing • 1 (800) 933-2667 • KaganOnline.com

ROUNDROBIN

ROUNDROBIN

In teams, students take turns responding orally.

ROUNDROBIN is a simple turn-taking structure. The teacher announces a topic, and each student in turn shares something with teammates. For example, the teacher may ask students to name as many adjectives as possible to describe the main character. An easy way to remember the name RoundRobin is break the word into two: "Round" means it goes around and each member gets a turn. "Robin" is a songbird that sings out. Each member gets a turn to sound off. The RoundRobin and RoundTable family of structures are among the most commonly used simple cooperative learning structures.

RoundRobin is flexible. It can be used to share just about anything. RoundRobin is used for teambuilding and getting acquainted, *"Share with the team your favorite thing to do on the weekend."* RoundRobin is used to share writing, *"Read your poem to the team."* RoundRobin is used for sharing opinions or perspectives, *"Is global warming fact or fiction? Why?"* RoundRobin is used to share answers, *"What did you write for question 1?"* RoundRobin can proceed in a single round with each teammate taking a single turn (Single RoundRobin), or there can be multiple rounds of RoundRobin—a Continuous RoundRobin. RoundRobin is a powerful tool in any teacher's toolbox.

THE POWER OF A ROUNDROBIN

Here are some of the many ways you can use RoundRobin.

- **Teambuilding**—Describe your favorite holiday.

- **Brainstorming**—Describe a drought-busting idea.

- **Prewriting**—Describe what you might write about.

- **Recalling**—Name and describe a type of cloud.

- **Processing**—Name a key point from the lecture.

- **Comprehension**—Describe one thing that happened.

- **Thinking**—Predict what will happen next.

- **Sharing Answers**—Share what you wrote for number 4.

- **Sharing Products**—Share your drawing.

- **Sharing Opinions**—Defend your favorite candidate.

- **Sharing Writing**—Share your story.

- **Making Decisions**—Name your preference.

BENEFITS

Students...

...share in their teams.

...receive equal turns.

...hear the ideas and answers of teammates.

...are held accountable to teammates for staying on task

Step 1 — Teacher Assigns a Task

The teacher assigns a topic or question with multiple possible answers and provides Think Time. *"In your teams, you will RoundRobin your favorite part of the book. When I say, 'Go!' you will start with the teammate with the longest hair and proceed clockwise. First, think about your favorite part."*

Step 2 — Teammates Take Turns Responding

In teams, students respond orally, each, in turn, taking about the same amount of time.

RoundRobin

STRUCTURE POWER

RoundRobin is the workhorse of cooperative learning structures. Together with its many related structures, for many teachers, RoundRobin is the most frequently used structure and has the greatest range of functions. As simple as it is, RoundRobin has all the elements of strong cooperative learning. Students are on the same side, encouraging each other. Each in turn is accountable for participating. Participation is equal. And a quarter of the class is responding at any moment. In the traditional class, the teacher calls on students one at a time to answer the question, "*What did the author want us to feel or think?*" In the cooperative learning class, the teacher asks the same question, but then has students do a Continuous RoundRobin.

In the same amount of time that the traditional teacher can call on and respond to three or four students in the class, each giving one answer, the teacher using RoundRobin has had every student in the class give several answers! The traditional teacher is always calling on those with their hands up—the high achievers. The cooperative learning teacher is calling on everyone. By calling more often on the high achievers in the traditional class, the achievement gap increases. By calling on all students equally in the cooperative class, the achievement gap decreases. Why call most on those who least need the practice and call least on those who most need the practice? Why call on one, when in the same amount of time, we can call on everyone?

TIPS

• **Stand Up.** Students stand when it is their turn so that everyone has a visual cue of whose turn it is to talk.

• **Pass It.** Visually indicate whose turn it is by passing an item, such as a microphone, ball, or conch.

• **Think Time.** Allow students several seconds of Think Time before the RoundRobin. Think Time is just 3–5 seconds of quiet time for students to think about their responses. Think Time encourages more responses and more thoughtful responses and is used frequently in the cooperative classroom where students interact with teammates about the curriculum.

• **Polite Listening.** Make sure to mention that no one is to speak out of turn. When it is not their turn, teammates are to practice "polite listening."

• **Right to Pass.** Students may need some more time to think about what they want to say or how they want to present. Rather than holding up the team, students can "pass" one round.

IDEAS Across the Curriculum

Mathematics

- Practice skip counting
- Practice times table, each stating a problem and answer
- Explain the steps of a proof in geometry
- Name things with right angles in the room
- Share your word problem
- Name ways to build 12
- Answer the next problem
- Describe one way to solve the problem
- Name next item in the pattern
- Define spatial terms
- Define geometry terms
- List odd numbers
- Estimate the likelihood of an event
- Make an inference from a graph
- Describe a real-world application

Language Arts

- What is your favorite story?
- Retell the story
- Retell the story without a character
- Retell the story with a major switch
- Give book reports
- Read creative writing and get input
- Predict what the book will be about
- List character trait adjectives
- State possible morals to the story
- List ideas to write about
- Provide feedback to a written piece
- Define literary terms
- Define story elements
- Evaluate a book
- Create a topic sentence for a paragraph
- RoundRobin Read— take turns reading story or book
- Read your poem
- Read your letter
- Read your descriptive story
- Read your persuasive paragraph

Social Studies

- List how the time of the Pilgrims was different from today
- Give famous people reports
- List things the executive branch does
- List a pro or con
- List a cause or effect
- Describe a Bill of Right Amendment
- Give opinion about a current event
- Give opinion about a social issue
- Describe one similarity or difference in the culture
- Describe one event in the time period
- Describe one prominent individual in the movement
- Estimate the distance
- Describe one outcome of the court case

- Offer one solution to pollution
- Define geography terms

Science

- Identify hot/cold items; list state of matter
- Science project reports
- Explain the stages of _____
- Things that float; things that sink
- List or describe elements
- Things that are in motion
- Sources of energy
- One use of electricity
- Things that stick to a magnet
- RoundRobin Read—take turns reading chapter or document
- Examples of a category (e.g., mammals)
- One difference between plant and animal cells
- Jobs scientists have
- Describe your hypothesis
- Properties of energy
- A principle of motion
- An observation from the experiment
- Ideas to save endangered species
- Natural disasters
- Define scientific terms
- Read your conclusions

Art

- Repeat the rules
- List a famous artist
- Share your artwork
- Define art term

Teambuilding

- Favorite food
- Favorite hobby
- Vacation I loved
- Music I listen to
- 3 wishes I have
- Favorite TV characters
- What are you most proud of?
- What did you do this weekend?
- What did you do over the break?
- What is the scariest thing you've experienced?
- Where would you like to go on vacation?
- What is your favorite meal?
- If you could be a professional athlete, what would be the sport?

Second Language

- People in the community
- Pronounce the voocabulary word
- List item of clothing

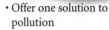

RoundRobin

VARIATIONS

• **Add Paraphrase Passport.** During RoundRobin or RallyRobin, the next student to share must first paraphrase the prior speaker before he or she has the "passport" to share.

• **Add Praise Passport.** During RoundRobin or RallyRobin, the next student to share must first praise the prior speaker before he or she has the "passport" to share.

RELATED STRUCTURES

#37 Continuous RoundRobin

Continuous RoundRobin is a RoundRobin that goes on for multiple rounds on the same topic. For example, the RoundRobin topic may be: "*Describe one event in the story.*" Since many events occur in the story, students can do round after round without repeating ideas. A Continuous RoundRobin is in contrast to a Single RoundRobin, where teammates only take one turn each.

Step 1 Teacher Assigns Topic

The teacher assigns a topic or question with multiple possible answers or provides a list of questions.

Step 2 Students Respond Orally

In teams, students take turns responding orally. The RoundRobin continues for multiple rounds until time is called or until a specified number of rounds are completeled.

#38 Rotating Role RoundRobin

Different roles can be added to RoundRobin, depending on the type of task. For example, students may brainstorm in RoundRobin fashion. The roles might be the following:

- **Idea Generator**—comes up with an idea.
- **Paraphraser**—states the idea in his or her own words.
- **Augmenter**—adds to the idea.
- **Cheerleader**—leads a brief celebration of the idea.

After each idea, teammates pass their role cards clockwise for the next round. Fan-N-Pick and Rotating Role Reading are two structures based on Rotating Role RoundRobin. Rotating Role RoundRobin is a highly-customizable structure based on a specific learning objective. The teacher selects the best four roles to perform the task at hand, and students rotate roles for each new problem or task.

Step 1 Teacher Assigns Task

The teacher assigns the task. Each teammate has a role card in front of them, relating to the task.

Step 3 Rotate Roles

Teammates pass their role cards clockwise for the next round.

Step 2 Teammates Take Turns

Each teammate takes a turn, preforming the role on the role card relating to the task.

#39 Single RoundRobin

A Single RoundRobin is a RoundRobin in which each teammate takes a single turn. For example, students may be asked to share their one best idea, one thing they did over the weekend, or their response to the question.

Step 1 Teacher Assigns Task

The teacher assigns a topic or question with multiple possible answers or provides four questions.

Step 2 Teammates Take Turns Responding

In teams, students take one turn responding orally. The RoundRobin is complete after each teammate has had a turn to share.

Timed Pair Share

#40 Think-Write-RoundRobin

The RoundRobin is preceded by Think Time and individual writing. For example, *"What did you have for dinner last night?"* or *"What do you predict will happen next in the story?"* Students think about their response and write it before they share with teammates. Including the think and write time before RoundRobin promotes deeper thinking on the topic. Students then develop their own ideas and are therefore less likely to simply copy a teammate's idea.

Step 1 — Teacher Asks Question

The teacher presents a question or assigns a writing (or drawing) task. For example, *"What made Alexander the Great so great?"*

Step 2 — Think Time

The teacher provides students a silent 3–10 seconds of Think Time to think of their responses. *"Everyone think about what you can write."*

Step 3 — Students Write

Students independently write (or draw) their responses. *"Write your own answer. No talking. Pencils down when you're done to signal you're ready for the RoundRobin."*

Step 4 — Teammates Take Turns Sharing

Students share their writing with their teammates, using RoundRobin.

#41 Timed RoundRobin

If the topic is sharing an opinion on something which may be time consuming, such as a project or creative writing, give teammates timed turns. Students may get 20 seconds for a short turn or 2 minutes for a long turn. If students finish before time is up, teammates can ask the student questions.

Step 1 — Teacher Asks Question

The teacher asks a question with multiple possible answers and states the time allotted for each response.

Step 2 — Students Respond Orally

In teams, students each, in turn, respond orally for the predetermined amount of time.

ROUNDTABLE

Structure #42
ROUNDTABLE

In teams, students take turns generating written responses, solving problems, or making a contribution to the team project that is passed around the table.

ROUNDTABLE is a fun and easy turn-taking structure. Students literally pass a list, story, or project "around the table," thus the name RoundTable. When it is their turn, each student makes a contribution to whatever the team is working on. If teams are creating a list of ocean animals, a pen and paper are passed around the table, stopping at each student as they add their animal to the list. If teams are generating a list of ideas, they pass the paper around and each student adds the next idea. If it is a team collage, each student in turn glues on the next piece.

RoundTable is good for mutual support and developing synergy in teams. Teammates all work on the same project and build on others' contributions. Students who otherwise might not contribute are held accountable for contributing.

DIFFERENTIATED INSTRUCTION

- Students can draw or select objects rather than write.
- Students can have a Scribe or aide write for them.
- Students can have guided practice on the content prior to the team RoundTable.

BENEFITS

Students...
...receive equal turns.
...see the contributions of teammates.
...build off other's contributions.
...work in teams toward a team goal.

59 Kagan Structures
Kagan Publishing • 1 (800) 933-2667 • KaganOnline.com

Step 1 Teacher Assigns Task

The teacher provides a task to which there are multiple possible responses and provides Think Time. *"In teams, come up with a list of adjectives in alphabetical order: amazing, beautiful, cuddly... . Pass a sheet of paper and a pen around the table clockwise. When the paper comes to you, write an adjective starting with the next letter."*

Step 2 Teammates Take Turns

In teams, students pass a paper and pencil or a team project around the team clockwise. On their turn, each teammate writes one answer or idea on the team paper or makes a contribution to the team project.

RoundTable

STRUCTURE POWER

RoundTable is the action counterpart of RoundRobin. In RoundRobin, students take turns talking; in RoundTable, students take turns doing something. Very young students may be passing around a basket, each adding something red from many items on the table. Older students may be passing around a copy of the periodic table, each filling in a bit of missing information. Young or old, students are learning more than the academic content. They are learning to work as a team, take turns, and appreciate the contributions of others. The power of RoundTable is in its flexibility. During one activity, students use RoundTable to build a tear-art clown: each in turn adding a piece. At another time, students use RoundTable to generate a written list of prime numbers. Later, they may pass around a Geoboard, each in turn building a geometric form by wrapping rubber bands around pegs on the board. There is hardly any academic content that can't be enriched by a RoundTable activity. Structures are like empty containers; to generate engaging activities, all we need to do is fill them with today's academic content. Tomorrow we fill that same structure with a very different content to create a different activity. Structures are activity generators.

TIPS

• **One Minute Rule.** One of the most common mistakes among teachers using RoundTable is to give tasks or questions that call for long responses. The longer the response, the more downtime for the other three students as they wait their turn. In creating RoundTable questions or tasks for students, it is helpful to remember the One Minute Rule: Every student should be able to respond within 15 seconds, so the project or paper makes it around the table in 1 minute. Longer responses usually mean too much downtime while the other three students wait their turn. For longer tasks, consider a Timed RoundTable or a RallyTable.

• **Use Colors.** Have each student use a different colored pen or maker when contributing to the team project. For papers that are turned in, students make a color key. This holds each student accountable for contributing and makes it easy to tell who did what.

• **The Right to Pass.** Students may need some more time to think about their contribution. Rather than holding up the team, students can pass one round.

• **Many Rounds.** Select topics or projects that can be completed in several rounds.

• **Level of Difficulty.** Since every teammate is performing without help, the team task must be easy enough for the weakest team member.

• **Short and Quick.** Tasks to which there are short quick answers keep the turn-taking process lively.

• **Add RoundRobin.** Have students say what they write or read what they wrote, so all teammates know what is written.

IDEAS Across the Curriculum

Mathematics
- Solve math problems
- Build a robot from shapes
- Measure angles
- Graph coordinates
- Write a bigger decimal
- Make patterns
- Do the next step

Language Arts
- Alphabetize words
- Make words from letters
- Define concepts: Love is…
- Identify parts of speech
- Add the next sentence to the story
- Spell the next word
- Correct sentences
- Add the next sentence to the answer

Social Studies
- Label states
- List countries
- Answer review questions
- List causes
- List an event that occurred
- Identify the capital
- List a law

Science
- List things found in the rain forest
- Identify objects in the Solar System
- Label bones
- Label muscles
- Label organs
- Label parts of a cycle
- Label a diagram
- Answer review questions
- Preform a procedure
- Do next step of the experiment

Art
- Creative drawing
- Collage
- Art project
- Draw the next item

Teambuilding
- Foods we like
- Songs we like
- Things we have in common
- Movies
- Items in your refrigerator
- Team projects
- Desserts we like
- Places we've been

RoundTable

RELATED STRUCTURES

#43 Continuous RoundTable

The team does multiple rounds of RoundTable until the teacher calls, *"Time's up,"* or until a predetermined number of rounds are completed.

Step 1
Teacher Provides Task

The teacher provides a task to which there are multiple possible responses, provides Think Time, and states time limit or number of rounds to be completed.

Step 2
Teammates Take Turns

Until the teacher calls, *"Time's Up!"* or rounds are completed, students pass a paper and pencil or a team project around the team, each taking a turn writing one answer or making a contribution when the paper or project comes to them.

#44 Pass-N-Praise

This is an add-on that can make almost any RoundTable variation more positive. Students pass their papers or projects to the next teammate. Teammates examine the prior teammate's contribution, then offer a praiser. For example, *"Oooh, I like that sentence!"* Then they add their own contribution. With each pass comes a praiser.

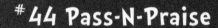

Step 1
Teammate Takes a Turn

A teammate takes a turn contributing to the team paper or project. When done, the teammate passes it to the next teammate clockwise.

Step 2
Praise

The next teammate reads the contribution and praises the contribution of the prior teammate. It might sound like, *"Great idea Kyle!"* or, *"I really like that you added eyes to the head."* After praising, the teammate makes a contribution to the paper or project.

Step 3
Repeat

Students continue praising, making a contribution, and passing until time's up or the task is complete.

#45 Rotating Role RoundTable

Teammates each perform a role, then, after each round, the role is rotated clockwise. For example, the roles may be Problem Solver, Coach, Checker, Cheerleader. The Problem Solver solves the first problem. The Coach offers help as requested. The Checker uses an answer sheet to check for accuracy. The Cheerleader leads the team in a celebration. Teammates then pass their role cards clockwise for the next problem. Roles differ for different types of tasks. For example, for descriptive writing, the roles might be Recorder, Modifier (who adds descriptive words or phrases), Checker, Cheerleader. For peer editing, the roles may have students check for: 1) spelling, 2) punctuation, 3) word choice, and 4) sentence structure.

Step 1 Teacher Assigns Task

The teacher assigns a task. Each teammate has a role card in front of them, describing their role as they work on the task.

Step 2 Teammates Take Turns

Each teammate takes a turn, performing the role on the role card relating to the task.

Step 3 Rotate Roles

Teammates pass their role cards clockwise for the next round.

Rotating Role RoundRobin vs. Rotating Role RoundTable

The difference between a RoundRobin and a RoundTable is a RoundRobin is oral and a RoundTable is written or involves another task such as contributing to a project. The difference between these two Rotating Role structures is the same: If it is oral, it is a RoundRobin. If it involves writing or doing, it is a RoundTable.

#46 RoundTable Consensus

Students must check for approval from teammates before they make their contribution. Teammates use a thumbs up signal if they approve or they place their hand flat on the table if they disapprove or feel the contribution can be improved. If teammates (one or more) signal with a hand down, the student may make the case for his or her contribution and the team discusses until they come up with an alternate contribution that is approved by all.

Step 1 Teacher Assigns Task

The teacher assigns the class a task to complete in teams. The task can be to write a team paper, create a team project, or complete a worksheet as a team.

Step 2 Teammate Begins

One teammate starts the team task. If the task is to complete a worksheet, the teammate works out the first problem aloud.

Step 3 Check for Consensus

The teammate who responded checks with the team for consensus. "*Does everyone agree that I solved it correctly?*" Depending on the task, the teammate may seek consensus before acting. For example, with a team project, the teammate may ask, "*Is everyone cool with me coloring the title red?*"

Step 4 Thumbs Up or Thumbs Down

Teammates show approval with a thumbs up, or if they don't approve, they place a hand on the table.

Step 5 Celebrate or Coach

If there is agreement, the students celebrate. If not, teammates discuss the response until there is agreement and then they celebrate. If students can't reach consensus, they can temporarily set the problem aside or postpone performing the proposed action. They can seek a different, mutually acceptable solution, or if it is a problem the team can't agree on how to answer, they can each raise a hand to signal the teacher they have a Team Question.

Step 6 Continue

The next teammate clockwise seeks consensus and answers or makes the next contribution.

#47 Simultaneous RoundTable

Simultaneous RoundTable increases active participation and the number of responses or contributions each teammate makes. Instead of one paper and one pen per team (or one project), in Simultaneous RoundTable there are four papers and four pens (or four projects). Each teammate makes a contribution to the paper or project in front of him or her. When time's up or when students signal they're ready, they each pass the paper or project to the teammate on the left for the next contribution.

Simultaneous RoundTable can also be used for worksheet work. Each teammate receives a different worksheet with problems. Students solve the first problem, then pass their worksheets clockwise. The next teammate checks the previous answer for correctness. If it is correct, they continue. If it is incorrect, the team stops and they coach. Each time the papers are passed, each teammate checks an answer and answers a new question.

Step 1 — Teacher Assigns Topic

The teacher assigns a topic or question and provides Think Time.

Step 2 — Teammates Respond

All four teammates respond to the worksheet or project in front of them, simultaneously writing, drawing, or building something with manipulatives.

Step 3 — Signal Time's Up

The teacher signals time, or students place thumbs up when done with the problem.

Step 4 — Students Pass Clockwise

Students pass papers or projects one person clockwise.

Step 5 — Students Add to Paper

Students check the current status of the project and make the next contribution. For example, if it is a story, students read what's going on in the story, then add the next part.

Step 6 — Repeat

When time's up, or when students signal they're ready, they pass papers or projects again. The process continues until students finish the projects, worksheets, or when the teacher calls, "*Time.*"

#48 Single RoundTable

The team does just one round of RoundTable.

Step 1 Teacher Assigns Topic

The teacher assigns a topic or question with multiple possible answers or provides four questions.

Step 2 Students Take Turns

In teams, one teammate responds first. The next teammate responds. The RoundTable is complete after each teammate has had one turn.

#49 Timed RoundTable

If the task is complex, provide a time limit for students to take their turn. For example, each student gets 15 seconds for their turn.

Step 1 Teacher Assigns Task

The teacher provides a task to which there are multiple possible responses, provides Think Time, and specifies the time allotted for turns.

Step 2 Students Take Turns

For the specified amount of time, students take turns passing a paper and pencil or a team project, each writing one answer or making a contribution.

SAGE-N-SCRIBE

SAGE-N-SCRIBE

In pairs, students solve problems, taking turns playing the roles of the Sage and the Scribe.

SAGE-N-SCRIBE maximizes overt active participation for problem solving. It converts monotonous problem solving into a socially engaging event. Students break into pairs, usually pairing up with their shoulder partners within their teams. One partner is the Sage and the other the Scribe. For the first problem, the Sage orally instructs the Scribe how to solve the problem step-by-step while the Scribe simultaneously solves the problem according to the Sage's instructions. For example, for the double-digit math problem 38 + 47, the Sage might say, *"First rewrite the problem with 38 directly on top of 47. Now add the ones column. Eight plus seven is fifteen. Write five under the ones column and carry the ten to the top of the tens column. Now add three plus four plus one. Write eight under the tens column. Our answer is 85."* If, while giving instructions, the Sage gives an incorrect instruction, the Scribe tutors the Sage. Tutoring is not telling answers or taking over, it is reminding the Sage of the procedure. When done with the problem, the Scribe praises the Sage, *"You add like a true mathematician!"* Students switch roles with each new problem.

In Sage-N-Scribe, the whole class is 100 percent actively engaged at any point. If we look at any pair, we see why: The Sage orally instructs the Scribe while the Scribe simultaneously carries out the Sage's instructions. Both students are simultaneously engaged. And that is true for every pair in the class. In addition, students have in their partners an immediate resource to help them work though the problems.

DIFFERENTIATED INSTRUCTION

Students may work in similar ability pairs and pairs may be given differentiated curriculum, difficulty levels, or time.

BENEFITS

Students...

...are optimally engaged for problem solving.

...verbalize their problem-solving strategies.

...are accountable to their partners for staying on task.

...have partners as immediate peer tutoring resources.

...receive immediate feedback and praise.

STEPS

Step 1
Sage Instructs Scribe

The Sage orally describes to the Scribe how to perform a task or solve a problem. For example, the Sage's instructions to the Scribe for correcting sentences for grammar might sound like this: *"To fix this sentence, first capitalize the first letter. Next, the word "their" is spelled incorrectly. It should be spelled t-h-e-r-e…"*

Step 2
Scribe Writes Solution, Tutors if Necessary

The Scribe solves the problem in writing according to the Sage's step-by-step oral instructions. If the Sage gives incorrect instructions, the Scribe tutors the Sage. *"I think we missed one. Let's look at the punctuation for the end of the second sentence."*

Step 3
Scribe Praises Sage

After completion of the problem, the Scribe praises the Sage. *"That's right, proper nouns should be capitalized. You aced that one!"*

Step 4
Partners Switch Roles

Students switch roles for the next problem or task.

Sage-N-Scribe

STRUCTURE POWER

The Common Core Curriculum calls for students to verbalize their thinking as they solve problems. How can they do that if they are seated in rows, solving worksheet problems alone? There are a number of advantages to having students verbalize their thinking in all content areas. As students verbalize their thinking, they listen to themselves. This reinforces their thinking and creates a greater probability of self-correction. Recent research on working memory demonstrates that the more we exercise working memory, the smarter we get. As the Sage verbalizes his or her thinking, the Sage is bringing thoughts into full consciousness, developing working memory. There are advantages in this process for the Scribes as well. The Scribe hears the thinking of the Sage. Because students are in heterogeneous pairs, the lower achieving partner has a positive model. Research on mirror neurons indicates that a primary way for students to learn is for them to hear and see a positive model. That higher achieving student in the pair is the positive model for the lower achieving student. During traditional worksheet work, some students have their pencils on the paper while their minds are far away. In Sage-N-Scribe, because one student is verbalizing the problem solving while the other is recording, their minds can't wander. In traditional worksheet work, some students think they are solving problems correctly when in reality they are making an error. They won't discover their error until the teacher has had time to grade the papers and get them back. By then it is too late because the student has finished the worksheet. The student does not have time to practice the corrected procedure. In Sage-N-Scribe, because feedback is given during each problem, corrections are immediate and students practice any correction they receive. Praise is yet another reason Sage-N-Scribe is so powerful. Research on retrograde memory enhancement demonstrates that anything associated with emotion is far more likely to be remembered. Praise follows each problem, creating emotion and cementing the learning into memory. Instead of having students working silently in isolation, during Sage-N-Scribe students receive encouragement, tutoring, and praise. Sage-N-Scribe makes practice an exciting, memorable experience. No wonder students love it, achievement goes up, and the achievement gap goes down!

TIPS

- **Shoulder Partners.** Students work as shoulder partners so that there is not too big of an ability gap. The high and low-medium students are shoulder partners, and the low and high-medium students are shoulder partners. Also, shoulder partners are better than face partners because with face partners one teammate has to read upside down.

- **Consult Teammates.** If the pair gets stuck on a problem or has a question, they can consult the other pair on their team. If the other pair doesn't know, each teammate raises a hand signaling to the teacher that they have a Team Question.

- **Model Roles.** Model for students the roles of the Sage and the Scribe. It is especially important to describe for students how detailed the Sage should be in providing oral instructions to the Scribe. The more precise the instructions, the better.

- **Sponge.** Pairs will finish at different rates, so have challenge problems, more problems, or a sponge activity ready for quick pairs.

- **Coaching.** Students need to learn what to do and say as a coach. They need to know that telling their partner the answer hurts the partner. They need instead to remind their partner of the rule or the procedure and have their partner apply it. It is helpful to model for students good and poor coaching before beginning Sage-N-Scribe, and have students define good coaching.

- **Appreciations for Coaching.** Give the students gambits to use if they receive coaching. Ask them, *"What do you say to your partner if they have given you some coaching?"* Have them generate gambits like, *"Thanks for reminding me." "I appreciate your help."*

IDEAS Across the Curriculum

Mathematics
• Compare decimals (.30 ____ .25)
• Long division
• Determine volume in cubic units
• Area in square centimeters (3 cm by 6 cm)
• Graph the following point (7, 4)
• Geometry proof
• Apply a formula
• Describe a rule for number pairs (40, 30; 23, 13; 52, 42 …)
• Reduce an answer to lowest terms (5/8 − 1/8 =)
• Write a word problem (126 ÷ 6 = 21)

Language Arts
• Fix the punctuation in a sentence
• Locate a word in a dictionary
• Use appropriate capitalization
• Fix an incomplete sentence
• Fix a run-on sentence
• Alphabetize a word or list
• Address an envelope
• Determine sentence tense (past, present, future)
• Define a word using context cues

Social Studies
• Locate state on map
• Ancient Egypt review
• Maya/Aztec/Inca questions
• Branches of government questions
• Civil war questions
• Explorer questions
• American colonies questions
• Map questions
• Latitude/longitude questions
• Landforms questions

Science
• Locate cell parts
• Label body parts
• Write bone names
• Categorize foods by group
• Research planet facts
• Mole conversion
• Molecular mass
• Oxidation/reduction
• Mitosis/meiosis stages
• Match mineral to definition
• Solve gravity problems
• Convert Celsius into Fahrenheit
• Word problems
• Convert kilos to pounds
• Classify organisms

Second Language
• Translate sentences
• Write directions
• Describe a picture
• Practice vocabulary

Sage-N-Scribe

Instructions. Find the area of each structure. Show your work.

1.

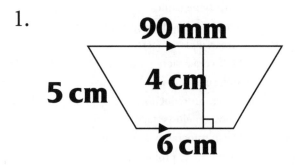

90 mm

4 cm

5 cm

6 cm

2.

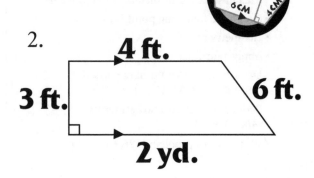

4 ft.

3 ft.

6 ft.

2 yd.

3.

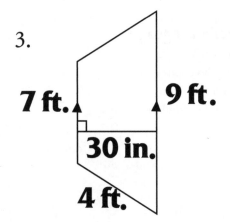

7 ft.

9 ft.

30 in.

4 ft.

4.

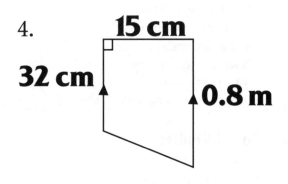

15 cm

32 cm

0.8 m

Answers:
1. 30 cm2
2. 15 ft2
3. 20 ft2
4. 840 cm2

SOURCE: Bride, B. *Cooperative Learning & High School Geometry.* San Clemente, CA: Kagan Publishing.

ORDER OF OPERATIONS
Sage-N-Scribe

Instructions. Perform the indicated operations.

1. $-5^2 - 8(-2)$

2. $-7(1-5)^2 + 1$

3. $10 - (-3)^2 + 5$

4. $8(-2) - 3^2$

5. $\dfrac{-3(2-4)}{-6}$

6. $\dfrac{-42(2)}{9-13}$

7. $11 - (5-2)^2 \div 3$

8. $6 - (8+1)^2$

Answers:

1. −9	2. −111	3. 6	4. −25
5. −1	6. 21	7. 8	8. −75

SOURCE: Bride, B. *Cooperative Learning & Pre-Algebra*. San Clemente, CA: Kagan Publishing.

MASS STOICHIOMETRY
Sage-N-Scribe

Instructions. These are sample chemistry Sage-N-Scribe problems.

1

$$C_2H_6 + O_2 \rightarrow CO_2 + H_2O$$

How many g of carbon dioxide are produced at the same time as 360 g of water vapor in the burning of ethane?

a) Balance _____

b) Giv/Req Given _____ Required _____

c) Solution

2

$$Na_2CO_3 + BaSO_4 \rightarrow BaCO_3 + Na_2SO_4$$

How many grams of sodium carbonate, Na_2CO_3, reacting with excess barium sulphate, $BaSO_4$, would be required to produce 85 g of barium carbonate?

a) Balance _____

b) Giv/Req Given _____ Required _____

c) Solution

SOURCE: Plumb, D. *Structures for Success in Chemistry*. San Clemente, CA: Kagan Publishing.

SHOWDOWN

Structure #51
SHOWDOWN

Students independently answer a question, then have a "Showdown" displaying their answers to teammates.

SHOWDOWN adds an element of fun and excitement to what otherwise may be considered boring drill and practice. Showdown replaces independent problem-solving practice. Showdown works best with high-consensus, right-or-wrong answers. First, the teacher assigns the class a set of problems to work on. For math, the problems may be adding mixed fractions. For language arts, the problems may be answering reading comprehension questions. Any practice or review problems work. The teacher then selects a "Showdown Captain" for each team. The Showdown Captain reads the first question. Teammates independently solve the problem or answer the question on their own AnswerBoards. They turn over their AnswerBoards, put down their pens, or give a hand signal when done. The Showdown Captain calls, "*Showdown!*" and all teammates show their answers. If students (one or more) hold up an incorrect answer, the team works together and tutors the student(s) needing help. Once they all know how to derive the correct answer, the Showdown Captain calls for a team celebration: "*Let's all do a team handshake!*" The Showdown Captain role is rotated around the team for each new question.

Showdown is the antidote to monotonous, independent problem-solving practice. Students enjoy Showdown. If a student needs help on any problem, the team knows immediately and they work together to tutor teammates who need help.

DIFFERENTIATED INSTRUCTION

- Similar ability groups may be formed to play with developmentally appropriate content or difficulty.

- The teacher, an aide, or a buddy may sit with and provide support for an individual student.

BENEFITS

Students...

...are accountable for working on each problem and sharing answers.

...receive frequent practice.

...receive immediate feedback.

...help each other when help is needed.

...have fun during drill and practice.

Getting Ready: *The teacher prepares questions or problems. Questions may be provided to each team as question cards that they stack face-down in the center of the table. Each student has a slate or a response board and a writing utensil.*

Step 1
Teacher Selects the Showdown Captain

The teacher selects one student on each team to be the Showdown Captain for the first round. "*Student #4 is the first Showdown Captain. Rotate the role clockwise after each question.*"

Step 2
Showdown Captain Reads a Question

The Showdown Captain reads the first question. If using question cards, the Showdown Captain draws the top card, reads the question, shows it to the team, and provides Think Time. "*Think about your answer.*"

Step 3
Students Answer Independently

Working alone, all students write their answers and keep their answers to themselves, hidden from teammates.

continued

Showdown

Step 4
Teammates Signal When Done

When finished, teammates signal they're ready by turning over their response boards, putting down their markers, or giving a hand signal.

SHOWDOWN!

Step 5
Showdown Captain Calls "Showdown"

The Showdown Captain calls, "*Showdown!*"

Step 6
Teams Show Their Answers

Teammates simultaneously show their answers and RoundRobin state them in turn.

Step 7 — Teams Check for Accuracy

The Showdown Captain leads the team in checking for accuracy. "*Great. We all got the same answer.*" Or, "*We did not all have the same answer, let's see how to get the right answer.*"

Step 8 — Celebrate or Coach

If all teammates have the correct answer, the Showdown Captain is Team Cheerleader. If a teammate or teammates have an incorrect answer, teammates coach the student or students with the incorrect answer, then celebrate.

Step 9 — Rotate the Captain Role

The person on the left of the Showdown Captain becomes the Showdown Captain for the next round.

Showdown

STRUCTURE POWER

Suspense fills the air at the end of a round of poker when there is a showdown, and we find out who wins the round. Also suspenseful was when gunslingers in the Old West faced each other, ready to draw their pistols for a showdown that could mean life or death. Suspense also fills the air when we play Showdown in the classroom: "*Will I have the right answer? Will all of us agree?*" The Showdown Captain calls, "*Showdown!*" And YES, we get to celebrate. Excitement is emotion and positive emotion translates into motivation and memory. Students are motivated to do the next round of Showdown because it is fun. Because there is emotion linked to the learning, there is memory for the learning. Rather than filling out a boring worksheet only to be evaluated later by the teacher, students are playing an exciting game and receive immediate feedback and correction, if necessary. Frequent, immediate feedback aligns with the basic principles of learning. The fun and excitement students experience as they play Showdown aligns with motivation theory and with brain-friendly learning principles. Showdown is powerful!

TIPS

• **Showdown Captain Card.**
Each team has a role card that says, "Showdown Captain." The role card is passed to the Showdown Captain for each new question, so everyone knows whose turn it is to act as the Showdown Captain. See blackline.

• **Right or Wrong Answers.** Showdown is ideal for practice and review. It works best with right-or-wrong answers that students can easily check for correctness. The answer can be folded inside a slip of paper to hide it. The slip is unfolded to check the answer. Or, the team can have an answer key to check for correctness.

• **Sequential Worksheets.** The team can do Showdown using problems from a worksheet or problems posted by the teacher. For worksheets that are sequenced by difficulty, students simply start at the first problem and progress sequentially.

• **Pick a Problem.** Showdown can be used with any questions or problems posted on the board or projected, or problems from a worksheet or book. To do this, the Showdown Captain picks from numbered cards corresponding to the questions displayed. The team answers the problem selected.

• **Question Cards.** Although any questions will work, Showdown is more focused and game-like when each team has their own set of question or problem cards that they turn over one at a time.

• **Showdown, Not Showoff.** Explain that the reason students compare answers is not to see who's better at that particular type of problem solving. It's not a contest. The idea is to get everyone to succeed: to find out who is having difficulty, and to try to steer them in the right direction.

• **Sponge.** Students may finish each problem at a different time. Have one or more sponge problems students can work on while waiting.

• **Response Boards.** Students can work on individual slates, dry-erase boards, or chalkboards. This makes it easy to show each other answers during the Showdown.

• **No Answer.** If students don't know the answer, they are allowed to put a question mark on their board, indicating that they need help with the problem.

• **Showdown Captain Plays.** The Showdown Captain answers every question, too. Being the Captain doesn't exempt him or her from solving the problems.

• **Think Time.** Before playing, instruct students on the importance of Think Time and how to patiently wait 3–5 seconds before writing.

IDEAS Across the Curriculum

Mathematics
- Place value
- Fractions
- Decimals
- Operations to use
- Order of operations
- Formulas
- Shapes
- Rounding
- Test questions

Language Arts
- Punctuation needed
- Vocabulary
- Parts of Speech
- Grammar
- Elements of a story
- Comprehension questions

Social Studies
- Questions from cultures
- Facts about Native Americans
- Definitions
- Historical characters
- Events
- Review questions

Science
- Weather
- Nonliving items
- Solar system
- Cloud formations
- Earth/rocks
- Formulas
- 5 senses
- Animal classification

Music
- Identify types of music
- Identify instruments
- Define terms
- Identify notes

Art
- Primary colors
- Elements of art
- Famous works of art
- Art history questions
- Art movements

Second Language
- Places in a city
- Food names
- Clothing
- Parts of the body
- Immediate family names
- Weather expressions
- Items found in a classroom
- Professions

Physical Education
- Flag football rules
- Muscles
- Volleyball rules
- Nutrition questions

Showdown

SHOWDOWN CAPTAIN CARD
Showdown

Instructions. Give each team a Showdown Captain Card. The student with the card is the Showdown Captain. The card is rotated one student clockwise after each problem.

SHOWDOWN CAPTAIN

1. Read question
2. Answer solo
3. "Showdown"
4. Celebrate or coach
5. Rotate Showdown Captain and card

SHOWDOWN CAPTAIN

1. Read question
2. Answer solo
3. "Showdown"
4. Celebrate or coach
5. Rotate Showdown Captain and card

SHOWDOWN CAPTAIN

1. Read question
2. Answer solo
3. "Showdown"
4. Celebrate or coach
5. Rotate Showdown Captain and card

SHOWDOWN CAPTAIN

1. Read question
2. Answer solo
3. "Showdown"
4. Celebrate or coach
5. Rotate Showdown Captain and card

RENAISSANCE
Showdown

Instructions. These are sample Renaissance Showdown cards to play Showdown.

RENAISSANCE 1

A. Who painted the *Sistine Chapel Ceiling*?

B. The *Mona Lisa*?

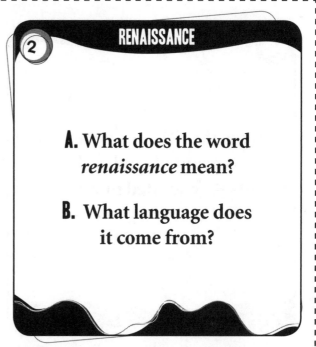

RENAISSANCE 2

A. What does the word *renaissance* mean?

B. What language does it come from?

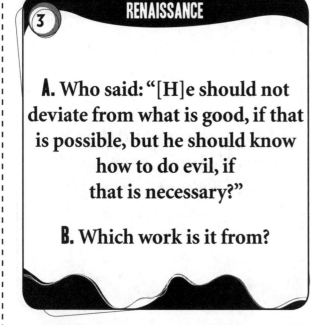

RENAISSANCE 3

A. Who said: "[H]e should not deviate from what is good, if that is possible, but he should know how to do evil, if that is necessary?"

B. Which work is it from?

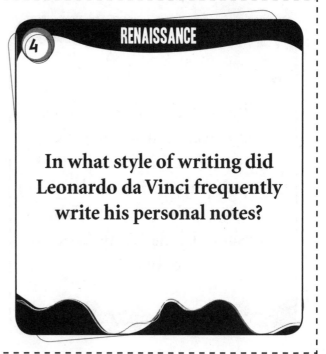

RENAISSANCE 4

In what style of writing did Leonardo da Vinci frequently write his personal notes?

ANSWERS:
(1) **A.** Michelangelo **B.** Leonardo da Vinci (2) **A.** rebirth **B.** French
(3) **A.** Niccolò Machiavelli **B.** *The Prince* (4) right to left, or "mirror writing"

 **MIDDLE AGES**

 Showdown

Instructions. These are sample Middle Ages Showdown cards to play Showdown.

---

① MIDDLE AGES

What is the title of a person who was granted land and the profits it generated in return for military allegiance to his lord?

---

② MIDDLE AGES

What was the main church during the Middle Ages in Europe?

---

③ MIDDLE AGES

What terrible disease killed about 25 million people (approximately one-third of Europe's population at the time) and was the subject of the nursery rhyme "Ring Around the Rosie"?

---

④ MIDDLE AGES

Which century did the First Crusade begin, starting with the Peasants' Crusade?

ANSWERS:

(1) vassal   (2) Roman Catholic Church

(3) Black Death or bubonic plague   (4) late eleventh century

DECIMALS INTO FRACTIONS TASK CARDS
Showdown

Instructions. Write each decimal as a fraction.

0.5	**0.25**
0.6	**0.20**
0.75	**0.8**
0.35	**0.05**
0.68	**0.16**

Instructions. Add the suffix *-ly* or *-ful* to each word.

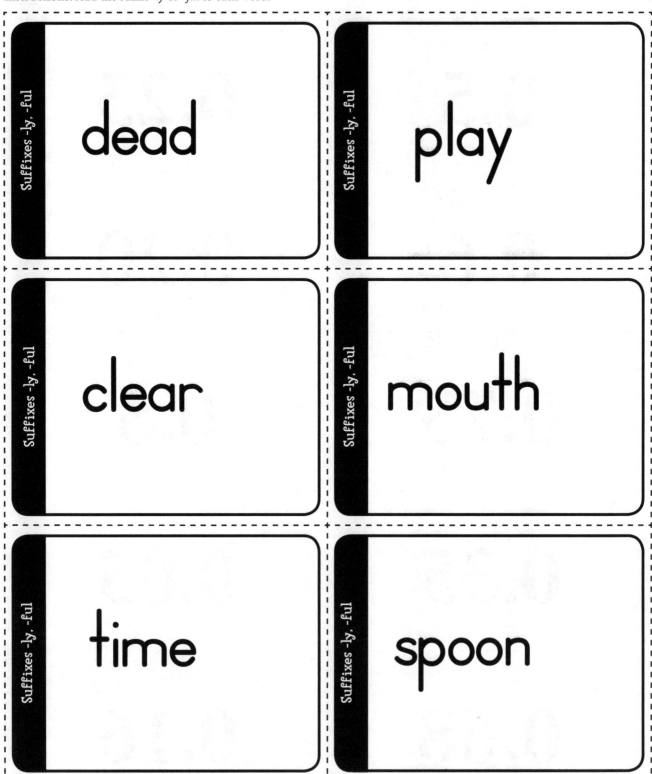

Suffixes -ly, -ful

dead

Suffixes -ly, -ful

play

Suffixes -ly, -ful

clear

Suffixes -ly, -ful

mouth

Suffixes -ly, -ful

time

Suffixes -ly, -ful

spoon

SOURCE: Skidmore, S. & Graber, J. *Balanced Literacy Grade 2*. San Clemente, CA: Kagan Publishing.

Instructions. These are sample Forces Showdown cards to play Showdown.

1 What is the definition of a force?	**2** What are unbalanced forces and how do they relate to motion?
3 What is the one result that occurs from friction?	**4** Which of Newton's laws makes the Space Shuttle fly and why?
5 How can Newton's first law be seen while driving a car?	**6** What is the equation for Newton's second law of motion?

SOURCE: Michels, M., Manzi, A. & Mele, J. *Cooperative Learning & Science High School Activities.* San Clemente, CA: Kagan Publishing.

COMPARE WHOLE NUMBERS
Showdown

Instructions. Cut out each card along the dotted line. Teams stack the cards facedown to solve using Showdown.

1 Put in order from least to greatest

2,304; 2,403; 2,334; 2,430

2 Put in order from least to greatest

5,002; 5,222; 5,200; 5,020

3 Put in order from least to greatest

43; 40; 29; 35

4 Put in order from least to greatest

401; 400; 410; 402

5 Put in order from least to greatest

55,434; 55,444; 55,400; 55,401

6 Put in order from least to greatest

101,256; 101,555; 101,562; 101,602

7 Put in order from least to greatest

32,978; 32,988; 32,977; 32,987

8 Put in order from least to greatest

73,653; 73,666; 73,573; 73,676

SOURCE: Stites, R. & Pfannenstiel, A. *Cooperative Math Grades 3–5*. San Clemente, CA: Kagan Publishing.

SIMILARITY GROUPS

Structure #52
SIMILARITY GROUPS

Students move about the room forming groups. They discover qualities of their classmates they did not know, and each student makes a special connection with at least one classmate.

THE TEACHER ANNOUNCES a topic and has the students think about the topic. Students then form groups—students with similar characteristics or values group together.

Similarity Groups is powerful for classbuilding. For example, students group by their favorite hobbies or favorite desserts. Similarity Groups can be used to form similar interest groups. For example, students group by topics they'd like to write a report on. Similarity Groups can also be used to explore academic content, such as grouping by most influential world leader or most difficult homework problem. And finally, Similarity Groups can be used for students to explore their own values and beliefs. For example, students group by the character virtue they most value.

Similarity Groups gets all students actively involved, energizing them while they learn more about themselves and their classmates. It is an excellent way for classmates to get acquainted. Students feel mutual support because they discover there are others like themselves. Similarities are the impetus for strong classmate bonds.

BENEFITS

Students...

...have fun getting acquainted and learning more about classmates.

...clarify their own values.

...see and appreciate individual differences.

...form friendships based on new-found commonalities.

...build a sense of belonging.

...become comfortable expressing their characteristics, values, and preferences.

...enjoy movement.

Step 1 Teacher Announces Topic

The teacher announces any topic on which students might group. The teacher guides students' thinking by providing imagery about the topic. *"Think about one of your favorite desserts. (Long pause.) Write down your favorite dessert."*

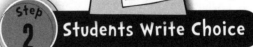

Step 2 Students Write Choice

Students think about the teacher's prompt and write their choice on a slip of paper.

Step 3 Students Form Groups

Students get up and move about the class, grouping with those with a similar response. If students can't find any classmates with a similar response, they form a new group called, *"Other."* *"When I say, 'Go,' I want you to get up and form groups. Group with students who like the same or a similar dessert."*

Step 4 Teacher Announces Discussion Topic

The teacher announces a discussion topic or question and provides Think Time. *"What do you most like about the dessert? How often do you have it? When was the last time you had it? Think about your response."*

Step 5 Students Interact in Pairs

Within their similarity groups, students pair up using Timed Pair Share, or Timed Pair Interview. *"Pair up with the person closest to you in your similarity group. Partner A's respond for 30 seconds, then Partner B's respond for 30 seconds."*

Similarity Groups

STRUCTURE POWER

One of the most important cognitive skills is the ability to categorize information. Throughout their lifetimes, our students will be faced with an accelerating information doubling-rate. Ability to categorize information is a survival skill for the 21st century. In addition to practicing categorizing, during Similarity Groups students have fun, get acquainted, and bond with classmates by solving a class challenge. The more often students do Similarity Groups, the smarter they are at categorizing and the better they like class. If the content is academic, *"Group by what you think is the most important line in the poem,"* students have also deepened their exploration of the topic. There is more power than meets the eye in simply having students get up and form Similarity Groups!

An occasional additional step to Similarity Groups has students recategorize their groups. Recategorizing promotes cognitive development. Students learn mental flexibility as they learn to look at the data and each other in different ways. This ability to look at the same thing in a fresh, new way develops "out-of-the-box" thinking.

TIPS

- **Write Group Name.** Have students write their preferences or characteristic before forming groups, so they don't group by friendship.

- **Similar Groups.** Students can join groups with others similar to themselves; they don't need to be exactly the same.

- **Quick Check.** Before all students have firmly formed groups, have groups announce who they are. This avoids two "apple pie" groups who do not find each other.

- **Triads.** Make interaction triads when the groups don't split evenly into pairs.

- **Equal Time.** Give students equal time to discuss in pairs.

- **Open Topics.** Choose a dimension so students can surprise you with the groups they form.

- **No Crowding.** Have groups spread out, standing away from other groups to avoid crowding.

- **Recategorize Groups.** After students have formed similarity groups, we ask students to group themselves again, but they are not allowed to use any of the categories they have already used. For example, after students form similarity groups by family cars, they are asked to recategorize themselves. On the first round, the students typically form groups like "Ford," "4x4," "Van," and "Toyota." On the second round, they are not allowed to use dealer labels, colors, or any of the categories they have already chosen. Typically, they recategorize themselves forming groups with labels like, "Needs a wash," "Has a dent," "Gas guzzler," and or "Has a sunroof." We have given students practice in categorizing information, in recategorizing the same information, and in breaking a common cognitive set. They are thinking out of the box.

IDEAS Across the Curriculum

Mathematics
- Favorite shape
- Hardest homework problem

Language Arts
- Genre
- Author
- Poet
- Story character
- Book

Social Studies
- Famous person
- Country (most like to vacation, live)
- Time period

Science
- Animal (favorite, like to be for a day, best pet)
- Technology profession
- Favorite technology
- Science profession
- Invention
- Plant
- Weather/climate
- Natural disaster

Music
- Instrument
- Song
- Band
- Soloist

Art
- Favorite color
- Favorite art form or style
- Artist
- Art period

Physical Education
- Sport
- Professional team
- PE activity to play
- Professional athlete

Classbuilding
- Type of shoe
- Pizza topping
- Soda
- TV program
- Fruit
- Vegetable
- Dream vacation
- Hobby
- Birthday month
- Restaurant
- Cartoon character
- Candy bar
- Disney character
- Car (color, make, thing they like most)

Similarity Groups

VARIATIONS

- **Choral Response.** Have students prepare a "We are..." Choral Response to announce their group. The statement can be a simple statement of the group's similar characteristic: "*We are the apple pie group.*" Or the group can be given some time to come up with a more creative statement: "*Nothing is more American than apple pie. And nothing tastes better than a hot slice with vanilla ice cream.*"

- **Whip.** After pairs share, let the class hear a sampling from each similarity group by randomly selecting one or two students from each group to share what they heard from their partner.

- **Paraphrase Partners.** After students listen to a partner in their similarity groups, they pair with a new partner with the group and paraphrase what the old partner said.

- **Dissimilarity Groups.** After students have formed similarity groups, have students form pairs or groups with students from different similarity groups. Give the group a discussion topic relating to their area of difference. This provides the basis for sharing and hearing different perspectives.

- **Pantomime or Skit.** With some content, Similarity Groups lends itself to an exciting pantomime game. For example, after grouping by their favorite sport, students can be asked to think of a way to show others their group choice using a pantomime (without talking) or with a brief skit. After acting it out, the other groups put their heads together and come up with their best guess. The acting group congratulates those groups who guessed correctly. Each group takes a turn acting out their group name.

Structure #53

TALKING CHIPS

Structure #53
TALKING CHIPS

Teammates place a "talking chip" in the center of the team table each time they talk. No one can talk again until all chips have been used, and teammates collect their chips for another round.

EACH STUDENT receives one "talking chip." The chips can be poker chips, pens, pencils, erasers, slips of paper, or any other tangible item. Students are given an open-ended discussion topic such as, "*What do you think about climate change?*" In order to speak, a teammate must place one of his or her chips in the center of the team table. At this point, it is his or her turn to speak. Teammates cannot interrupt the speaker; they practice respectful listening. When the speaker is finished, another student places his or her chip in the center of the team table and is free to add to the discussion. When a student uses his or her talking chip(s), he or she cannot speak until all teammates have added to the discussion and placed their chip in the center of the table. When everyone has had a chance to speak, students collect their chips and continue a new round using their talking chips.

Talking Chips regulates discussion, ensuring that everyone participates. Everyone gets the opportunity to speak their mind. Each contribution is valued, and if a time limit is imposed, no single student can dominate the team discussion.

DIFFERENTIATED INSTRUCTION

Selected students may be given time to read about, think about, and/or talk about the topic prior to playing Talking Chips.

BENEFITS

Students...

...each get a turn to speak and are accountable to teammates for contributing.

...contribute spontaneously, as there is no predefined sequence.

...participate more equally.

...cannot interrupt; they practice respectful listening.

...who are shy are encouraged to participate.

Step 1
Teacher Announces a Topic

The teacher announces the discussion topic to the class and provides Think Time. *"Who do you think is the more qualified candidate and why? Think Time."*

Step 2
Any Teammate Starts

Any teammate begins the discussion, placing one of his or her chips in the center of the team table.

Step 3
Continue Discussing

Any student with a chip continues discussing, placing his or her chip in the center of the team table.

Step 4
Start the Round Again

When all chips are used, teammates collect their chips and continue the discussion using their talking chips.

Talking Chips

STRUCTURE POWER

Years ago, as a research professor, I conducted an experiment to study social interaction patterns. I took sheets of colored cardboard and cut one-inch squares of four different colors. I gave students discussion topics like "*If we could add 10 minutes to lunch time or to recess, which would you prefer, and why?*" For older students it was questions like "*Do you support capital punishment? Why or why not?*" I put students in groups of 4, gave each student 10 chips of their own color, and gave them 6 minutes of discussion time. I instructed them to place their chip in the center of the team table each time they talked.

The pattern was the same among young and old students: In many groups, red would go in, then blue, then red, then blue, occasionally green, and yellow never. I then tried the experiment again, but changed the rule: You get one chip each and once you use it, you cannot talk again until all chips have been used and collected for a second round.

The pattern changed dramatically: All students participated about equally. Talking Chips was born! What became obvious from these experiments was that an unstructured team discussion is just like giving every student as many chips as they want. The result in many groups is very unequal participation. If we want to equalize participation, we need to structure for it. Talking Chips is a very simple structure with powerful results. Students who would usually let the others take over find their own voice!

An added, unexpected benefit of Talking Chips turned out to be more focused listening. Students and adults report they listen more carefully when Talking Chips is used. After using their chips, they do not focus on what they want to say next, but rather on what the speaker is saying.

TIPS

• **Talking Police.** Assign one teammate the role of the Talking Police. The Talking Police's job is to make sure no one talks without a chip to spend.

• **Any Chip Will Do.** Any tangible items will work as Talking Chips: pencils, pens, crayons, erasers, tokens, poker chips, checkers, etc.

• **No Order.** Unlike most structures, Talking Chips has no prescribed order. Tell students they can participate when they have something to add as long as they have a chip.

• **Colored Chips.** Colored chips can help the teacher and teammates monitor who's talked and who is yet to contribute.

• **Discussion Time Limit.** The teacher can set a time limit for the discussion to get all teams to end at the same time.

• **Timed Talking Chips.** If some students are talking too long with a single chip, set a time limit for how long you can speak with one chip. A Time Monitor can use a team timer to clock each contribution.

• **Freebies.** Students can respond yes or no to questions without giving up a talking chip.

IDEAS Across the Curriculum

Mathematics
- Strategies for solving a problem
- Shapes around the room
- Ideas for a math project
- What are real-world examples of this type of math?

Language Arts
- Story conclusions
- Improvisational drama
- Discuss main ideas
- Answer open-ended questions
- Favorite parts of a story
- What would you change about the story?
- Summarize the book
- Give your interpretation of the poem
- Similarities and differences between characters

Social Studies
- Topics for team reports
- Discuss events and effects on history
- How can we make the world a better place?
- Advantages/disadvantages of a democratic society?
- The similarities and differences of people or cultures
- What can we do about the water shortage?
- Was Nixon a good president?
- Should torture be legal?
- Should presidents have term limits?
- Should guns be outlawed?
- Should the U.S. maintain its embargo against Cuba?
- Solutions to illegal immigration
- Should we have pre-emptive wars?
- Similarities among religions
- Different customs
- Should there be campaign spending limits?
- Should all citizens have access to health care?

Science
- Discuss a field trip
- Discuss current events—cloning
- What do you know about _____?
- What is the most interesting thing you learned about _____?
- What did you learn from the chapter?
- What generalizations can you make from this experiment?
- Describe your own experience with a natural disaster
- Should euthanasia be legal?
- Summarize the safety procedures
- Should we genetically modify food?
- Ethics of cloning
- Should animal testing be legal?
- How could we stop the spread of ebola?

Music
- What instruments do you hear in the piece of music?
- What is the best band of all time?
- What is the best type of music and why?

Art
- What comes to mind when you see the picture?
- Evaluate the art
- Is photography art?

Teambuilding
- Which cartoon character is like you?
- If you were a superhero, which superpower would you want?
- If you had 1 week to live, what would you do?
- Describe the people in your family
- Describe your hobbies
- Describe your perfect spring break
- Should students be allowed to use cell phones at school?

Talking Chips

VARIATIONS

• **Finger Count.** Students discuss the issue or topic in teams. Instead of using chips to speak, they raise the number of fingers on a hand to indicate how many times they've contributed. For example, after each teammate contributes once, they all hold up one finger. The rule is, you can only speak again and increase the number when all teammates are on the same number. For example, no student can speak for the second time until all teammates are holding up one finger.

• **Gambit Chips.** Gambit chips have sentence starters to direct responses. For example, if students are working on paraphrasing skills, the gambits may be "*You believe...*" or "*If I hear you right...*"

• **Paraphrase Passport.** Students can share their own ideas only after they accurately paraphrase the person who spoke before them: "*You said that...*"

• **Praise Passport.** Students can share their own ideas only after they praise or affirm the person who spoke before them: "*I like how you said...*"

• **Yarn Yarn.** Young students wrap a piece of yarn around their wrist each time they talk. At a glance, students and the teacher can see the students' interaction patterns. Teams can reflect on the equality of participation and plan how to make it more equal.

• **Topic Chips.** To help guide the discussion, the chips can have topics relating to the discussion topic. For example, if the discussion topic is, "*Summarize the story,*" the chips can be character, plot, theme, or climax. When a student uses a character chip, he or she describes a character in depth.

Instructions. Cut out and use these chips for Talking Chips.

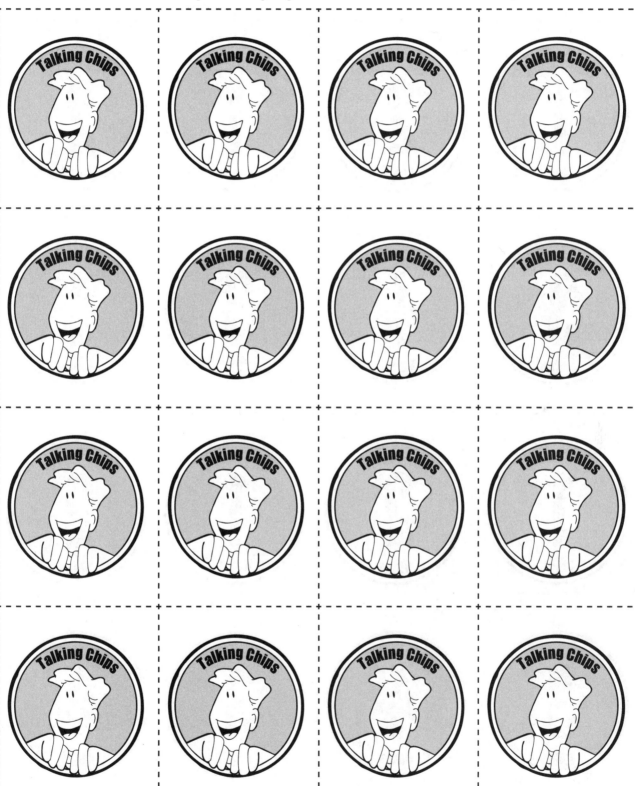

TURN-TAKING CHIPS
Talking Chips

Instructions. Each teammate gets four chips. No teammate can move on to turn two until everyone has used their chip for turn one.

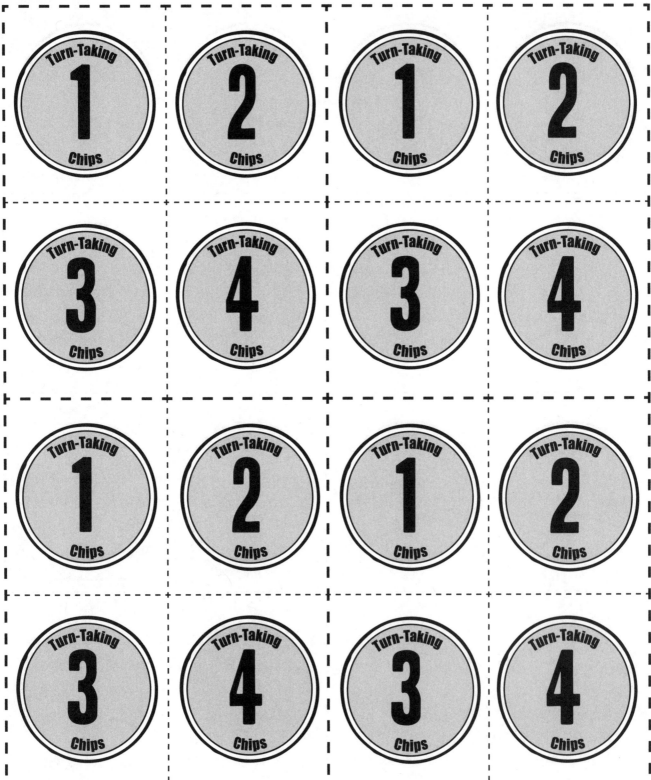

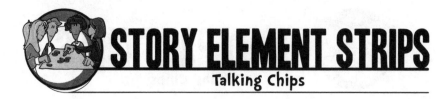
Instructions. Use these topic strips to discuss the elements of the story you read.

CHARACTER

SETTING

PLOT

PROBLEM

SOLUTION

STORY PART CHIPS
Talking Chips

Instructions. Use these chips to discuss the parts of the story.

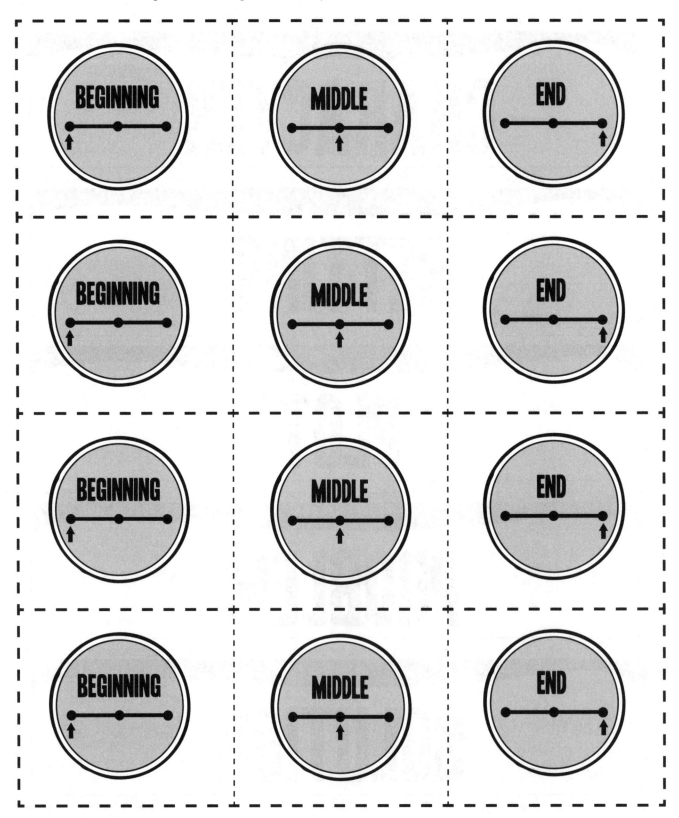

TEAM INTERVIEW

Structure #54
TEAM INTERVIEW

Each teammate experiences both sides of the interview coin: They are interviewed by three teammates at once and also act three times in the role of interviewer.

THE TEACHER introduces the interview topic. The topic can be a fun teambuilding topic such as, "*Find out what your teammates did over the weekend.*" Or the topic can be academic such as, "*Interview your teammates about their assigned reading.*" Team Interviews are also great for role playing. Students are assigned different characters from a story or different figures from a historical period, and teammates interview them in that role. For example, "*Mr. Churchill, what was your greatest accomplishment as prime minister?*"

In each team, one student stands to be interviewed. Teammates interview the standing student for 1 minute (or whatever time limit is set). When time is up, teammates appreciate the interviewee. The interviewee sits and the next student clockwise stands to be interviewed. The Team Interview is over after all students have been interviewed and are seated.

DIFFERENTIATED INSTRUCTION

- If they are to be interviewed in a role or about a topic, students can choose who they will be, or the topic.
- Students can be given the interview questions in advance and be given time to prepare their responses.
- Selected students can be given the opportunity to practice their responses with a partner, aide, or teacher in advance of the Team Interview.
- If they are to read about their interview topic, students can be given different ability leveled and interest leveled content and readability.

BENEFITS

Students...

...learn interviewing skills.

...learn to ask open-ended questions and follow-up questions.

...get a chance to interview and be interviewed.

...hear the ideas and experiences of teammates.

Step 1
Teacher Announces a Topic and Time Limit

The teacher announces a topic on which students are to interview each other. *"Find out your teammates' favorite after school activity. Interview each teammate for 2 minutes."*

Step 2
Teammates Interview the First Student

One student stands up. He or she is the first interviewee. Teammates can ask the teammate any questions they want.

Step 3
Teammates Appreciate Interviewee

When the interviewee's time is up, teammates thank the interviewee, and he or she sits down.

Step 4
Remaining Teammates Are Interviewed

The student to the left stands up and becomes the next interviewee. The Team Interview continues until all students have been interviewed.

Team Interview

STRUCTURE POWER

What power there is in a simple structure! It transforms an academic activity that ordinarily would take hours so that it takes only minutes—and with even more positive results! Let's say we want each student in the class to give a book report or a current event. The traditional teacher has each student present to the class for 3 minutes. The teacher is obligated to give the student feedback: praise and, if necessary, correction. That takes about 1 minute. Now comes the transition. The student who has presented walks back to their seat while the next student to present comes to the front of the room. That takes another minute. We are at 5 minutes per student. With 30 students in the class, a 3-minute book report each takes 5 x 30 or 150 minutes. Three class periods! How have the students spent their time? Only 3 minutes of active engagement and most of the rest of the 150 minutes with their minds wandering! Now let's say the teacher knows the power of Team Interview. The teacher has the students each give their 3-minute book report or current event in teams of 4. Following each report, each student is asked questions by teammates for another minute. This totals 4 minutes per student. After 4 x 4, or 16 minutes, the teacher has accomplished what it would have taken 150 minutes to complete using the traditional approach. How have the students spent their time? 3 minutes actively engaged giving their report, but far more engaged in the remaining time because they are asking or answering questions. Students listen more intently because they know they will ask teammates questions. Almost full-brain engagement for the entire time. With so much time saved, we can afford to give book reports, science reports, project reports, and current events far more often because they take 16 minutes—not 150 minutes—and students are engaged the whole time! What power there is in a simple structure!

TIPS

Pre-Made Questions. Announce the topic and have the class or teams generate interesting questions before the interview begins.

• **Time It.** Set 4 minutes on a countdown timer. The Timekeeper lets the team know when 1 minute has elapsed and that it is the next student's turn. At the end of the allotted time, all teams are done. Interval timers are ideal for Team Interview.

• **Open-Ended Questions.** Teach and practice with students how to ask open-ended questions to promote elaboration and avoid short answers.

• **Right to Pass.** The interviewee has the right to pass on any question he or she does not feel comfortable with. He or she just may say "*pass,*" or a silly code word such as "*hamburger,*" and the team asks the next question.

• **Teach Interviewing Skills.** Good interviewers come prepared with an interview agenda, but great interviewers know how to modify and adjust their questions, based on the responses. Analyzing a good TV or radio interview is a great experience for students.

• **RoundRobin Questions.** If students aren't participating about equally, you can equalize participation by having each teammate ask their questions in RoundRobin fashion (taking turns).

• **Questions I Want to Answer.** If a student gets a question and does not want to answer, the student has the option of responding to a question that he or she would like to be asked.

• **Stand Up.** Having the interviewee stand up helps the team focus on the interviewee. It also provides a visual management cue for the teacher to ensure students are switching roles on time. When the interview is done, all students are seated.

IDEAS Across the Curriculum

Mathematics

- If you could have any math-related job, what would it be?
- What do you like most about mathematics?
- What do you like least about mathematics?
- Where does mathematics rank compare to other subjects/classes?
- Finish this equation: $M + X = Y$. What are X and Y?
- Do you think the U.S. should use the metric system?

Social Studies

- Are you in favor of corporate bailouts or not?
- Do you think Oswald really shot JFK?
- If you were the president, would you have invaded Iraq after 9/11?
- Is war ever justified?
- Do you consider yourself a good citizen?
- Which American hero do you admire most?

Science

- Do you think the money invested in the space program is money well spent?
- If you could be a doctor, what type of doctor would you be?
- Can science and religion co-exist peacefully?
- If you could devise an experiment to get the answer to a question, what would your question and experiment be?
- What genes did you inherit from your dad?
- What genes did you inherit from your mom?

Art

- Describe your painting?
- Would you like to be a cartoonist?
- What is your favorite sculpture?
- If you were a photographer, what would be your subject matter?
- Complete this sentence: Beauty is…
- What is your impression of the art of this culture?
- Do you prefer realism, surrealism, or impressionism? Why?

Physical Education

- Which sport do you think is the most difficult?
- Are you more of a team player or an individual athlete?
- Are you more of a sprinter or a distance runner?
- Do you prefer doing weight training or aerobic exercise?
- What makes someone a good team player?
- Which athlete do you most admire and why?

Teambuilding

- Where is the most exotic place you've ever been?
- How many brother and sisters do you have?
- If you could have anything for dinner tonight, what would it be?
- What is your dream job?
- Would you rather be rich or famous?

Team Interview

VARIATIONS

• **In Role Interviews.** Students are each assigned a role, such as a character from a book they just read or a historical figure from the era they're studying. They answer the interview questions in that role.

• **Personify It.** Each teammate is assigned an inanimate object, theory, or principle. Students are interviewed in the role of that item and are to bring it to life for teammates.

• **Two Questions.** Rather than using a time limit, use a question limit. Each student must ask the interviewee two questions before he or she may sit down. This equalizes participation among interviewers.

PLANNING SHEET
Team Interview

Instructions. Write questions to ask your teammates during their turn being interviewed.

INTERVIEWEE #1	INTERVIEWEE #2	INTERVIEWEE #3
Name _____	Name _____	Name _____
Questions to ask…	**Questions to ask…**	**Questions to ask…**

ANSWER RECORDING SHEET

Team Interview

Instructions. Use this sheet to record what you learned while interviewing each teammate.

INTERVIEWEE #1	INTERVIEWEE #2	INTERVIEWEE #3
Name_____	Name_____	Name_____
Things I learned…	**Things I learned…**	**Things I learned…**

Structure #55

TIMED PAIR SHARE

Structure #55
TIMED PAIR SHARE

Partners take timed turns listening and sharing.

TIMED PAIR SHARE is one of the simplest cooperative learning structures—and one of the most powerful. The teacher states a discussion topic, how students are to pair, and how long students will have to share, and selects who will go first. After each student shares, his or her partner responds. As simple as it is, Timed Pair Share implements the basic principles of Cooperative Learning into just about any point of any lesson and for any objective. It can be used as a set, *"What do you predict this book will be about? Face partners share for 30 seconds each. Partner with the darkest clothes begins."* It can be used as a frequent processing break during a lecture, *"Turn to a partner and take turns sharing the key points of the lecture so far. You have 1 minute each."* Timed Pair Share can be used for quick group processing during a cooperative project, *"Pair up with someone on your team. How is your project going? Partner A share how well the team is staying on task. Partner B share how well the team is working together for 30 seconds each, go!"* It can be used for teambuilding, *"Share with your shoulder partner for 30 seconds what you did during the break. The student with the shortest hair starts first."* Or for classbuilding, *"Pair up with a classmate who is not a teammate and share what you did this weekend. Partner with the darker hair goes first: 1 minute each."* Timed Pair Share can be used to develop thinking on any topic, *"Partner A, how did the author convey the theme of the book? Partner B, how did the protagonist change or grow? Take 2 minutes each, Partner A starts."* Timed Pair Share is a staple in the cooperative, interactive classroom.

When you compare Timed Pair Share to its traditional counterpart—selecting one student to share with the class—its true power is revealed. With Timed Pair Share, half the class is active at any one time while the other half listen attentively. In the traditional class, only a single student in the whole class is active, while the many other students often tune out. With Timed Pair Share, no students get left behind. Everyone participates. Plus, students practice speaking and sharing their thinking, comprehension, and opinions. They learn to take turns. They practice listening attentively. A single Timed Pair Share versus selecting one student in the class probably doesn't add up to much, but when you consider how often we as teachers ask questions every day and then multiply that out by the number of days in the school year, this simple structure has the power to single-handedly revolutionize classroom teaching.

DIFFERENTIATED INSTRUCTION

Once the topic is announced, students may be allowed to prepare in their own way for the Timed Pair Share. Some may prefer to express themselves with a drawing, poem, rap, or mind map, or to act something out.

BENEFITS

Students...

…are actively engaged either sharing or actively listening.

…regularly express themselves.

…must participate.

…take turns.

…practice respectful listening.

…actively listens so they may respond appropriately.

…hear classmates' thoughts on the content or issues.

…make personal connections to the curriculum.

Step 1 — Teacher Asks Question

The teacher asks a question that students may elaborate on, states how long they will have to share, and provides Think Time. "*What do you already know about snakes? You will each share for 30 seconds. Think Time.*"

Step 2 — Partner A Shares

In pairs, Partner A shares while Partner B listens without talking. "*Partner A, please share your response for 30 seconds. Partner B, you are listening carefully, no talking.*"

Step 3 — Partner B Responds

The teacher tells Partner B how to respond. The response can be simply to "copycat" the teacher's response:
- "*Thanks for sharing!*"
- "*You are simply fascinating to listen to!*"

The response can be to "complete a sentence" starter such as:
- "*One thing I learned listening to you was…*"
- "*I enjoyed listening to you because…*"

Or the response can be a spontaneous response by the listener.

Step 4 — Switch Roles

Partners switch roles. Partner B shares while Partner A listens, then Partner A responds.

Timed Pair Share

STRUCTURE POWER

Timed Pair Share offers an instructive illustration of the power of structuring. Structuring makes the difference between learning for all versus learning for some. Contrast the outcomes of two structures that appear quite similar: One actually accelerates the achievement gap, whereas the other decreases the achievement gap and boosts achievement for all. Let's see how.

Knowing that writing improves when students talk about their ideas before, two teachers decide to allow students some "air time" before they do their creative writing assignment. One teacher has students in pairs and gives them 4 minutes, saying, "*For the next 4 minutes I want you to discuss your stories and be sure to talk about your characters, plot, setting, and conflict.*" The other teacher does a Timed Pair Share, giving each student in the pair 2 minutes to share their ideas for characters, plot, setting, and conflict.

If we observe students during the pair discussion, in every or almost every case, the higher-achieving student does most, or even all of the talking. In essence, without intending, the teacher has given an opportunity for the high achiever in each pair to articulate their ideas far more than the lower achiever. In a pair discussion, those who least need the benefit of elaboration get the most. Conversely, those who could most benefit from active participation get the least. In a Timed Pair Share, all students participate equally; all students are engaged. The achievement gap decreases, and achievement overall increases because the least participative, lowest-achieving students post dramatic gains when they are now actively involved with each other and with the curriculum.

TIPS

• **Think Time.** Give students at least 5 to 10 seconds of Think Time to think about what they will share.

• **Listen Up.** Tell students to listen carefully because you will ask them to paraphrase or respond to their partner. Occasionally, call on a student to share what his or her partner said.

• **Time It.** Use a visible timer so that students know when their time is up. Students can manage their own time better if they too can see the time elapsing.

• **Adjust Talk Time.** If students don't have enough to talk about for the time allotted, shorten their talk time. If you're cutting them short, lengthen the talk time.

• **No Interruptions.** Timed Pair Share is not a pair discussion. One partner does all the talking while the other only listens. Work with students to practice active listening.

• **Brainstorm Response Gambits.** Have students brainstorm response gambits. Post the gambits for all to see and use as they respond to their partners.

• **Mix Up Partners.** Have students talk with their shoulder partners at times and their face partners at other times. Have students occasionally pair up with classmates beyond their teams.

• **Finish Early.** If a student finishes before his or her allotted time is up, it is his or her partner's responsibility to ask related questions.

• **Who Goes First?** Make Timed Pair Share more game-like by using a random partner spinner, or flipping a coin to see who goes first. To save time when using a student characteristic to decide who goes first, use something visible rather than something that would take discussion or might sidetrack the discussion.

  • **Fast.** Tallest, shortest hair, larger hand, closest to the front of the room, has their next birthday soonest.
  • **Time Consuming or Sidetracking.** Lives farthest from school, has more siblings, hours you watch TV a night, number of video games you own, has traveled farthest on a trip.

• **Encourage Elaboration.** Don't ask questions students can answer with a yes or no or a short answer. Instead of asking, "*Who was the main character?*" ask, "*How would you describe the main character?*" Prompt students to elaborate, not to simply respond.

IDEAS Across the Curriculum

Mathematics

- Ways to solve a problem
- What is your definition of _____?
- Hardest part of about last night's homework
- What type of math would you use in the grocery store?
- How would you use this in everyday living?

Discussion Topics

- How might you use this in your life?
- What was the easiest/most difficult for you?
- How are these two equations different?
- How would you solve this problem?
- What are the characteristics of this shape?

Language Arts

- Predict the ending of a story
- Explain parts of your writing you like
- How is the main character like or unlike you?
- Prewriting
- What is the main idea?

Discussion Topics

- If you were to write a letter to this character, what would you say?
- What do you think this book will be about?
- What would the sequel of the book be about?
- What will happen next in the story?
- How did the setting influence the story?

Social Studies

- Explain a political cartoon
- How are we like/unlike _____?
- What do you enjoy doing in your community?
- What would you take on a wagon ride west?
- What new "right" would you add to the Bill of Rights?

Discussion Topics

- How are you like or dislike a historical character?
- What are your feelings about this current event?
- Would you like to live in this time period?

- Was he a good U.S. president?
- How is this culture similar to our culture?

Science

- Predict the results of a scientific experiment
- Derive animal characteristics
- Explain your experiment
- Favorite season, and why?
- Is evaporation important, and why?
- Cloning or ethical issue

Discussion Topics

- If you were to do this experiment again, what would you do differently?
- How has this animal adapted to its environment?
- Why is recycling important?
- What are some safety concerns related to this lab activity?
- What is more threatening: pollution or deforestation?

Art

- Favorite color, and why?
- Favorite artist, and why?
- What about what are you working on do you like best?

Physical Education

- Effects of good/poor health habits
- Favorite indoor game
- Favorite sport

Classbuilding

- Favorite part of school
- Which animal would you be for a day, and why?
- Summer fun
- Learned this year
- Which movie star would you be?

Timed Pair Share

VARIATIONS

· Progressive Timed Pair Share.
Partners take turns sharing on the same discussion topic for progressively shorter (or longer) time periods. For example, the pair starts with 2 minutes each, then get 1 minute each for the next round, then 30 seconds each for the final round. The number of rounds and time periods depends on students and the discussion topic.

· Stroll Pair Share. Students walk around the classroom in pairs as they each share on the assigned topic.

RELATED STRUCTURES

#56 Gossip Gossip

To increase active listening to their partners, tell students in advance to listen carefully to what their partner has to say because they will need to remember it. After pairs have shared both ways, students pair up with a new partner. Then, as if gossiping, they point to their old partner and gossip about what their partner shared. For example, "*Eugene said that the most interesting fact about the pronghorn antelope is that it is the fastest land animal in North America and can reach speeds of over 50 miles an hour and can maintain its speed for miles, whereas the cheetah can reach speeds up to 70 miles an hour but only for short bursts.*"

Step 1 Partners Share

Partners pair up and each take a turn sharing information with a partner.

Step 3 Students Gossip

Students share what they learned from their last partner.

Step 2 Students Find New Partners

Students pair up with a new partner. If they originally paired with their face partner, now they pair with their shoulder partner. Or, do a StandUp–HandUp–PairUp to have students pair with a classmate.

Step 4 Partners Continue

Students do multiple pairings, each time sharing what they heard from their last partner.

#57 Timed Pair Interview

The teacher provides the interview topic and states the time allotted for the interview. Partner A interviews B. "*Partner A is Abraham Lincoln. Partner B will interview the President for 3 minutes.*" When done, Partner A interviews Partner B. If they are interviewing each other in roles, Partner B may be assigned a new role.

Step 1 Teacher Provides Topic

The teacher provides the interview topic and states the time allotted for the interview. "*You will interview your partner for 2 minutes to find out what your partner knows about volcanoes.*"

Step 2 Think Time

The teacher calls for Think Time. "*Think about what you learned about this topic. Think about what questions you can ask your partner.*"

Step 3 Partner A Interviews Partner B

Partner A interviews Partner B.

Step 4 Students Switch Roles

Partners switch roles: Partner B interviews Partner A.

ABOUT ME QUESTION CARDS
Timed Pair Share

Teacher Instructions. Use these questions to have students do Timed Pair Share with classmates.

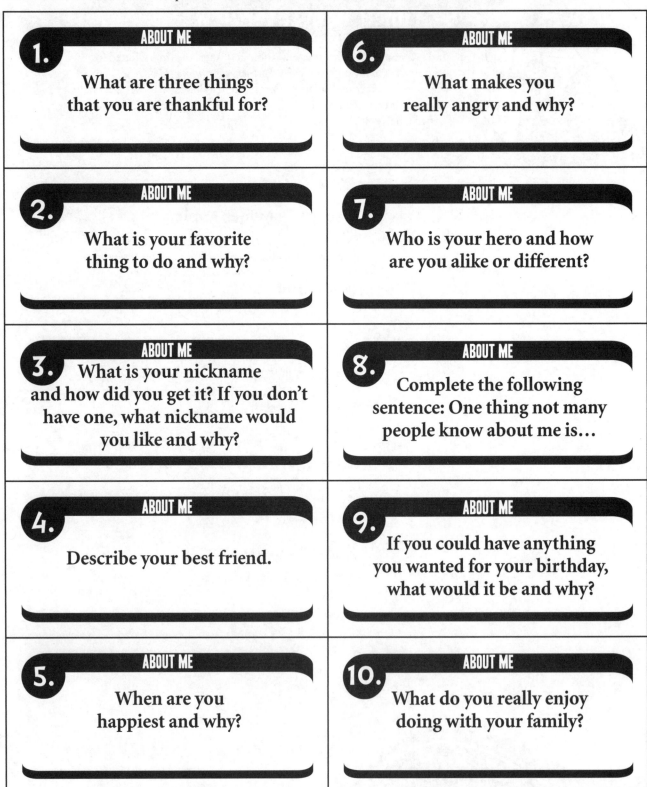

ABOUT ME
1. What are three things that you are thankful for?

ABOUT ME
6. What makes you really angry and why?

ABOUT ME
2. What is your favorite thing to do and why?

ABOUT ME
7. Who is your hero and how are you alike or different?

ABOUT ME
3. What is your nickname and how did you get it? If you don't have one, what nickname would you like and why?

ABOUT ME
8. Complete the following sentence: One thing not many people know about me is…

ABOUT ME
4. Describe your best friend.

ABOUT ME
9. If you could have anything you wanted for your birthday, what would it be and why?

ABOUT ME
5. When are you happiest and why?

ABOUT ME
10. What do you really enjoy doing with your family?

SOURCE: Kagan, S. & Kagan, M. *Kagan Cooperative Learning.* San Clemente, CA: Kagan Publishing.

CHARACTER QUESTIONS
Timed Pair Share

Teacher Instructions. Use these questions to have students do Timed Pair Share with classmates.

Character Questions **1** Who is your hero? What traits or qualities does he or she have that you admire most?	**Character Questions** **6** What does the following quote mean: "Stand for what's right, even when you stand alone"?
Character Questions **2** How would you define the word *character*?	**Character Questions** **7** Is morals the same thing as values?
Character Questions **3** What character trait do you value most? Why?	**Character Questions** **8** "Character is who you are and what you do when no one else is looking." Do you agree with this quote? Why or why not?
Character Questions **4** Describe a book you've read that has a message about the importance of character.	**Character Questions** **9** The famous civil rights activist Martin Luther King, Jr. said, *"I look to a day when people will not be judged by the color of their skin, but by the content of their character."* Why should we judge others by the content of their character rather than by how they look?
Character Questions **5** Think of a movie you've recently seen. Is the lead role a person of high or low character? Give examples to support your claim.	**Character Questions** **10** There are absolute rights and wrongs that every person should know about. Do you agree or disagree?

SOURCE: Kagan, M. *Higher-Level Thinking Questions for Character Development.* San Clemente, CA: Kagan Publishing.

Timed Pair Share

Teacher Instructions. Use these questions to have students do Timed Pair Share with classmates.

Rain Forest

1 Have you ever been to a tropical rain forest? If so, describe it. What did you like best? If not, would you like to visit one? What would you want to see most?

Rain Forest

2 What would happen if the tropical rain forests of the world were cut down?

Rain Forest

3 Do you think natives to the rain forest have the right to do as they please with the land of the rain forest, or should they have laws? Explain.

Rain Forest

4 What can you do to help save the rain forests?

Rain Forest

5 Are you more like a toucan, howler monkey, jaguar, or sloth? Explain.

Rain Forest

6 How do you think the daily life of a rain forest native is different from yours? How is it similar?

Rain Forest

7 What are three reasons people would want to clear rain forest land?

Rain Forest

8 List five products that come from the rain forest.

Rain Forest

9 The rain forest is sometimes called the "lungs of the earth." What is another good metaphor for the rain forest?

Rain Forest

10 Rain forest land is often cleared for raising cattle. What is an alternative?

SOURCE: Kagan, M. *Higher-Level Thinking Questions for Character Development*. San Clemente, CA: Kagan Publishing.

TRAVELING PAIR SHARE

Structure #58
TRAVELING PAIR SHARE

Students pair up with classmates to share.

STEPS

Getting Ready: *Post multiple discussion questions on the board or give students a handout with multiple discussion questions.*

Step 1 — Students Pair Up

Students stand up, put a hand up, and high five to pair up with a classmate.

Step 2 — Partner Reads Question

One partner reads one of the posted discussion questions. For example, *"What engineering principles apply to a suspension bridge?"*

Step 3 — Other Partner Answers

The other partner answers the question.

59 Kagan Structures
Kagan Publishing • 1 (800) 933-2667 • KaganOnline.com

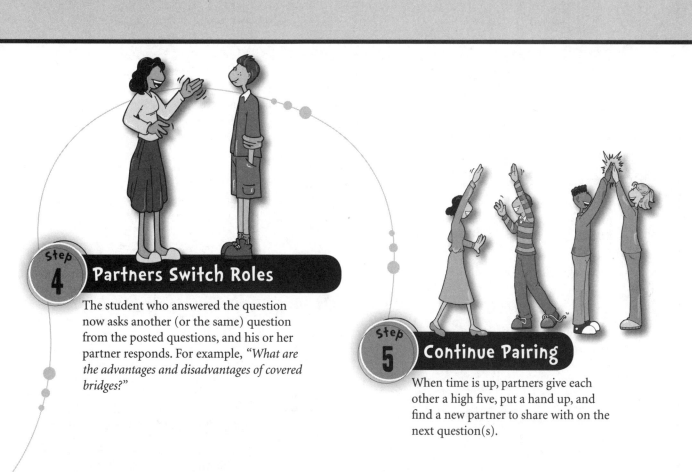

Step 4
Partners Switch Roles

The student who answered the question now asks another (or the same) question from the posted questions, and his or her partner responds. For example, *"What are the advantages and disadvantages of covered bridges?"*

Step 5
Continue Pairing

When time is up, partners give each other a high five, put a hand up, and find a new partner to share with on the next question(s).

#59 Invisible Pal

Students prepare by investigating, reading, or selecting an "Invisible Pal" (examples: element from the periodic table; multiplication fact; current or historical event; historical, contemporary, or literary figure). Students may take notes about their invisible pal. Students stand with their notes, a paper, and pen. Each student puts a hand up and pairs up with a classmate. Partner A in the pair introduces their invisible pal to Partner B, who takes notes. Partners switch roles: Partner B introduces his or her pal to Partner A, who takes notes. Partners thank each other and trade invisible pals. Students put a hand up and pair up with a new partner. The process is repeated a number of times with students always introducing a new invisible pal—the new pal is introduced to them by their last partner. The teacher calls time. Students return to their teams, taking turns describing and comparing notes about the invisible pals they met.

Students Research Topic

Each student is assigned a topic to research. For example, each student could be assigned a different animal. Students learn all they can about their research topic.

Students Pair Up

Students stand up, put a hand up, and pair up with a classmate.

Partner A Introduces Pal

Partner A in the pair introduces their "Invisible Pal" to Partner B, who takes notes.

Students Switch

Partners switch roles: Partner B introduces her or his pal to Partner A, who takes notes.

Pair Up With New Partner

Partners thank each other for sharing, then put a hand up and pair up with a new partner.

Repeat Process

The process is repeated a number of times with students always introducing a new invisible pal—the new pal is introduced to them by their last partner. The teacher calls time after students have paired many times.

Students Return to Team

Students return to their teams, taking turns describing and comparing notes about the invisible pals they met.

NOTES

NOTES